PRO-DOMME

by Aleta Cai

FOREWORD

I never had a guidebook, a mentor, nor any sort of practical advice when I entered into this industry. As much as I went looking for resources and how-to's, the ones I did find weren't very helpful. The books I found talked loosely about how to use various implements but didn't tell me how to get from A to B. What I really needed was to know what to watch out for, how to keep myself safe and step by step what to do.

I realized then that this career was something I had to jump into and learn through experience. The end result was rocky and although it worked for me, I would bet that this approach failed for many, many others. It's one of those tough positions where you often have to play not to lose until you can play to win. Through this work we're coming up against the law, against the often "dark" side of human nature and our own boundaries in ways our world cannot possibly prepare us for. I remember so many moments of fear, doubt, crisis, confusion and worry throughout — moments when I didn't know what to do next or if I'd make it to the next step at all. But, there was always one certainty. Domming was the one thing that kept calling me, that waited there for me again and again to come back even when I ran. It was always there for me even when other doors closed. I think when it comes down to it, as human beings we all want something unconditional, like love.

I thought to compile a guidebook for all of you who want to enter into this industry, who are curious about this industry, or who are already in it and looking for more guidance. In writing this, I thought about all of the information I wish I was told early on so that you have all the ins and outs at your disposal. There are too many stories of things gone wrong and I want to share what I know so you ladies have a good, safe and fun experience. You'll start to see that even though this is dungeon, BDSM specific, these are larger life lessons that have a thorough and wide application. The dungeon to me wasn't just a dungeon, it was a new perspective on life.

When I entered this industry, one of the first things I learned was how much turn-over there is. In my interview, I asked the dungeon headmistress if she thought I'd be able to do this work. At that point in time, although captivated, I was also struck by a debilitating amount of anxiety over what this work could do to my life as a whole. I didn't think I had it in me. I was then, conditioned by my culture and by my overly-dominant and traditional mother, to be submissive. I believed that men needed to lead and I needed to get out of the way, which is often a deep seated conditioning that happens to most women in a patriarchal culture. Although I was strong willed, I was also conditioned to doubt my instincts, intuition and my own ability to lead. Coming from most of my life spent in an all-girl's school and with a distant, scary and narcissistic father, men were fascinating, yet I couldn't begin to unravel them at all. To make matters worse, I was so shy, so scared, and so tied to my cultural conditioning of what was acceptable and "ladylike". Ladylike in conservative terms usually means disconnecting from essential parts of you, like your sexuality, your needs and your opinion and replacing them with guilt and shame.

The headmistress replied, "yes. Your measurements are good and you have an interest in psychology. It's the girls with an interest in psychology that usually stay. Most girls leave within 2-3 months," she said it so blankly, like she was Siri and just assessing various data she'd pulled up on google. It was so jaded that I knew she must've seen hundreds of girls come and go, knowing not to invest any heart into anyone.

Back then, I was looking for an answer more specific to me. Maybe she could've said, "you have a particularly fetishized look," or "your voice and young appearance would be great for turning the tables scenarios," so I would at least know which direction to go and what to highlight, but instead, it was just my proportions and my intellectual proclivities. These were so general. "That's all it takes?" I thought. "Could I literally just stand in a room, be myself and I'd be fine?". It was interesting how, even though this was a headmistress, I was leading the conversation and asking the questions. As soon as I arrived it was like I already had the job and she was trying to court me and only because I had the right measurements. I found it all so strange, considering I expected the opposite. I thought it would be an elusive, secret-society where the mistress would walk in in a latex catsuit with a slave on a leash, crawling behind her. She'd have a refined elegance and a seductive dominance that would make me fall to my knees in intimidation. Nope, it was far from that. The real headmistress wore a baggy, ripped t-shirt and sweatpants. She laughed a lot and wouldn't make eye contact. That was a lesson I'd learn again and again: this isn't glamourous. This is the opposite. It's gritty, it's realer than real, it's sometimes what you wish you could un-see.

When I left the dungeon and considered going independent, I wasn't sure if I was made out for it. I remember having tea with an established domme at the time. I exposed my worries about being too empathetic, and she told me it would be my million dollar trait. At the time I was confused as I saw my own empathy as a weakness. She also said she was sure I would make it as long as I continued to work on myself. It's often what people refuse to work through, their own shit, that ends up stopping them from succeeding.

Although at the time I didn't understand, I'm really glad she said what she did. I already had all I needed. It was just learning how to make the adjustment to see my weaknesses as strengths and then making the choice to work on them until they did become my strengths, that would determine if I had a future in this career.

You too have all you need. But if you want to grow, it's a whole different story especially in an industry that's as oversaturated as it is now. My evolution became one in which I was a shame-stricken domme at a boutique dungeon who, although found comfort, familiarity and freedom in the dungeon, thought that this was just an experience to be written off when I'd pursue a "legitimate" career. Then I became an independent domme who lives and breathes this work but still struggled with the cohesion of work and life. I alternated between fixating on the work to putting it aside for months at a time. Finally, I began utilizing the lessons in BDSM as a bridge to my life calling and artistic expression. That has opened the most doors. Although I don't consider myself a traditional domme at all, I realize that's the beauty of this work. It becomes what we make it.

I'm about to share with you the most important lessons I've discovered as a domme then, and since. and for those who have already been practicing, perhaps this can add another perspective. It's always amazing to meet other women in this work, because we all end up making it our own. In the end, dommes are artists. If you can't make it your own, then who are you? To make this resource easier to digest, I've also broken it down into categories:

The Practical: how to go about becoming a domme

General Advice: the broader lessons

Good luck, stay safe and be strong.

*Disclaimer: throughout this book I'll mostly refer to subs as he/

him only because I'm writing from my past experiences in which all of my former subs were men. The dungeon only permitted us to session with men. This is not meant to be discriminatory in any way, it's just the reality of my basis of knowledge.

If any illegal activities are mentioned, they're in the context of what was observed in the past and knowledge accrued from those experiences. My current practice is for holistic healing only and does not comprise of illegal activities. This is a guide purely for women to succeed as a professional domme, which as a profession is legal. All women who pursue domming and use this guide are assumed to be of legal age.

THE PRACTICAL

How do you start becoming a domme?

F irst step is: make sure this is right for you. Think on it for some time and work out any resistance you may be feeling. If it's a gut feeling of "no, this is wrong" then don't do it. If it's a feeling that there's fear blocking you, yet something is calling you, go for it.

Make sure you're willing to deal with the consequences, because there are real consequences to this work in a world that doesn't fully accept it yet. There are sacrifices to be made and you may need to give up certain friends or even a way of living. I've heard stories about former dommes who were outed and then fired from their place of work. This work follows you, especially when the internet keeps all traces of you. You may think that you have nothing to lose when you're young, but you always have something to lose. Even though life can change and it's hard to plan, you can too, so make sure to think about this decision carefully even if you don't know the outcome. Be prepared to let go of things, people, and even a version of you you've grown attached to.

For some of you, you'll never face the ostracization I did and maybe you come from a completely different background and social circle where this can be lived out in the open without any consequences.

Regardless, this industry is a tricky one being that it's so unregulated, and yet, so regulated. Especially now not just with Sesta and Fosta, but because even social media platforms are targeting sex workers and shadow-banning, or just plain deleting accounts for what counts as "solicitation". In this day and age, social media isn't frivolous, it's sometimes the basis of our entire business.

As a pro-domme, you have two options: you can either work at a dungeon or become an independent.

If you decide a dungeon's the way to go, now that backpages is no longer (that's how I found my dungeon) just do a search for dungeons in the area. Contact a few to see if anyone's hiring and meet the owners. Make sure that they're respectful and you align with their treatment of employees. Keep your power and don't jump into employment at the first place that takes you. Some dungeon owners can be sketchy or exploitative so be aware. Some even require free sessions from you which is a strange practice in my opinion. From here, you can always go independent when you're ready, or stay at the dungeon for the duration you're a domme.

Or you can go the mentorship route and look for dommes in the area that you respect and resonate with. Reach out respectfully, inquiring whether they're taking on mentees and what their fee is for training. Understand that if they do take time out to mentor you, they are sharing valuable information that took time and money to accrue so be appreciative and grateful. Never come across entitled or like they owe you something, because frankly they don't. With a mentor, that's a more direct path to being an independent domme.

◆ ◆ ◆

Is it better to stay at a dungeon

or to go independent?

I started out in a boutique dungeon that gave me a good understanding of the basics, but also taught me many things I needed to unlearn. You'll come to see that techniques aren't refined at most dungeons unless you're under the tutelage of a very skilled domme. When you're in a dungeon, usually someone else is booking for you and therefore you won't connect with every sub you see. There's a sense of being a service-top (more on this later) and there's more chance of burn out because of the high volume of clients. The house takes a portion (usually around 50%) of your money.

The pros are: you have a go-to space for work. You'll usually have all the implements and supplies provided by the house. You have a built in support system (that is, if the environment fosters a sisterhood rather than a competitive atmosphere) and you also don't have to take the full responsibility if something goes wrong. You have the dungeon to fall back on so this is a safety net as you're learning the ropes. There were some things that were fundamentally toxic about the dungeon I worked at, but in retrospect I'm incredibly thankful. I picked up so many skills I wouldn't have otherwise and had hands on help to build those skills.

I've met dommes who never worked at commercial dungeons and instead got a mentor. I've heard of a few women who found amazing mentors and because of this, got a unique access point. If you pick a mentor who is established, then likely you'll understand BDSM in a deeper way than what you can see at a dungeon. Because there are so few top-tier dommes and out of those few, I'd bet only a handful are accepting mentees, that path may take a long time. Then, I'd think that they'd be able to teach you their specialties, but it's still up to you to find ways to learn what they don't teach you. No one is an expert in everything.

Personally, I'd recommend starting at a dungeon because it'll give you a broad understanding of the basics and of various styles. It can introduce you to many different clients too. Then you'll be exposed to a wider spectrum and that in itself is priceless. **Remember: exposure is priceless because then you learn your limits, your likes and dislikes. This is a foundation for your career, no matter whether you stay a dungeon or become independent later.**

Also remember that who you receive training from is teaching you their style, so hopefully in your evolution you develop your own style. There isn't just one way to do any of this.

◆ ◆ ◆

Do I have what it takes?

Yes you have what it takes! Despite the sex industry making it seem like there's only one body type, despite what your dungeon or headmistress/master might tell you (my headmistress had a strict BMI and look she wanted the girls to strive for- I find this to be poisonous) what makes you YOU is what ends up earning you money. When you brand, always aim to highlight what sets you apart.

Luckily in BDSM there are so many different fetishes, kinks and archetypes. Therefore there's room for different looks and personalities. No matter your body type, look or interests, someone's going to fetishize you. The more unique you are, the more fetishized you can be, point blank.

If you're a softer, more nurturing personality, you'd be great at coddling or infantilization sessions.

If you're a cruel and punishing alpha, great! There's already such a big niche for you. There's a reason the classic, or "stereotypical" domme is the controlling, assertive and bossy one.

If you're young, great! You'll likely use this as an asset in your role-plays that require younger roles, like a schoolgirl. If you're older, that's wonderful, because there are many boss and teacher role plays for you.

If you're more playful than cruel, no problem. Many people want to escape into a fantasy that's fun and tap into their playful nature. There's a reason sessioning is called "play" afterall.

No matter what your personality is like, what your energy is like, what you're body is like, you're going to attract the right people to you if you put that out there. Just make sure you have a basic understanding of what you're putting out there, or, if you have no idea, take a look at what types of clients you're attracting to you and use this as intel. Ask your subs questions about what appeals to them about you. Adjust your branding and marketing accordingly.

If you have one or more specific features that set you apart, always photograph them.

I find that with BDSM, it's inclusive. Yes, we play into certain boxes and prototypes sometimes, but in the end there's a place for all boxes even the ones that society deems inappropriate or "perverse". In fact, in this space being a "pervert" can be a positive. I feel that sessions can serve as a healthy outlet because if someone's exploring something considered "wrong" in a safe context, consensually with an age-appropriate person, then they're not repressing, subliminating or exploring it in the real world in a way that may be unhealthy or damaging.

For instance, I used to work with a domme who looked very young and innocent. Some of her clients had fantasies about her being underaged (which she wasn't). She'd always say, "it's a good thing they're playing this out with me than doing this to a real underaged girl,"

◆ ◆ ◆

Do I need an alias?

Yes- most girls create an alias. If you start out at a dungeon, management will ask you to create one. If you're independent, for safety it is good to have an alias, not to mention it creates a separation between this work and your real life if you're not interested in integrating them just yet. Most people starting out don't yet, and I'd advise you to keep them separate until you're sure this is what you want to do with your life.

Think of it as an alter-ego. BDSM is not just an escape for the client, but for you as a domme it can offer an alternate reality where you get to be a version of you that you don't get to be elsewhere. An alias helps with that, as it suddenly snaps you out of who "you", or, your programmed identity that comes with so many ideas of who you can and can't be, to a clean slate. It can be such a relief, not to mention, a blank slate can be just what you need to start figuring out who you really are.

Pick whatever you want! My dungeon wanted me to pick a surname that matched my ethnicity, so I searched on wikipedia until I found one that resonated with me at the time. Later when I went independent, I also chose from the same list. With my first mistress identity, the dungeon picked my first name, one that I didn't like that much. This is like getting a tattoo. Make sure it's one that you like because you might have it on you for a while. Still, don't get too caught up in meaning because some people get tattoos that mean something deep and other people get tattoos simply because they like them. The interesting thing here is that even if it means nothing to you now, it may later.

◆ ◆ ◆

How do I write a bio?

T he second thing the dungeon asked of me was for me to write a bio for my page before I even started sessioning or had any sense of my style. Back then, I wrote something terribly cliché, but over the years it started to ring more true than I could've possibly known. I still use parts of my first ever bio in my ads now. I made a reference to healing and surprisingly, it became what I grew into. I didn't know I was a healer nor that BDSM could even be healing back then.

Your first bio doesn't need to be perfect. It can be cliché, especially as you figure out who you want to be in the territory. Word of advice: DON'T copy another person's bio. They will find out and they won't like it. You want your bio to be unique even if it is a bit cliché and superficial initially.

Write about your interests and what brought you into BDSM. A little backstory helps to engage your potential subs. Many dommes describe themselves physically, or encased in fantasy. You can write this to be a very tantalizing description of you, you can write it in third person as if you're a character in a book or movie like I did in my first take, you can describe your services, or you can write a straightforward one that describes you and what drives you in BDSM without bells and whistles.

I will say that many people use so many lofty descriptors and that

15

sometimes comes across as overcompensating. In many writing style books, they advise you to avoid using too many adjectives because they can clutter the main idea. My advice is just be straightforward, bold but real. When it comes down to it, the people that I've connected to in my years of practicing were those that appreciated my authenticity. That being said, authenticity is not what everyone gravitates towards. Some people are more turned on by distant fantasy and some women feel safer cloaked in that, too.

It can help to figure out what fantasy you elicit first. Ask your friends, subs or people you've dated and/or are dating. Are you a femme-fatale? Are you a girl next door? You can even explore archetypes in Robert Greene's infamous <u>The Art of Seduction</u>. Then utilize this information. For instance, the femme-fatale would be best to be more distant, as mystery, seduction and the space for projections serve her. The girl next door is more approachable. Tailor your bio accordingly. It doesn't hurt to make mention of these classic "roles" or famous people who played these roles, either, as that primes your subs and sets their expectations immediately.

Ex: "Like Marilyn Monroe..."

◆ ◆ ◆

How many hours is typical for a domme?

For a newer domme in a house, you're likely to be booked a lot in the first few months. Dungeons already have an established roster of clients and most of them are interested in the "new girl". I was booked back to back when I first started, even during training. My first two or three months were lucrative but be prepared for bookings to dwindle after that because of a few factors. If you aren't taking care to keep clients, if you aren't evolving in your skill set (if you're just coasting based on looks) or some outside factor like the dungeon happens to hire one or a few new dommes, then you're definitely going to experience less bookings. Even if none of these scenarios happen, your bookings may dwindle naturally as you lose your newbie status. Don't worry though, you're always likely to get more clients especially as the industry begins to open up more to the mainstream. Not to mention, there are always those legendary regulars that try out new dommes for the sake of it.

I made many mistakes at the beginning of my career. I didn't save my money, I just expected things to be as lucrative as they were, I got the dreaded mistress-itis (more on this later) and didn't think to retain my clients. I didn't pursue it seriously enough to expand my repertoire and instead took a passive approach. Still, I did well for the majority of my time in a dungeon. On the days I was on schedule, on average I did about 3-4 sessions a day. That's when I didn't care that much and I was one foot out the door. Girls that made this their full time career for years were booked back to back with weekly regulars and 4-5 sessions a day with recurrent overnights.

Now, I've thoroughly lessened my frequency. Although I invest more in my BDSM career and in my sessions, because they're super niche I don't often find the right fit. Not to mention, I keep my phone off, I don't reply to text messages and I rarely respond to emails. I book purely by intuition, which isn't how most dommes do this and isn't a business-y practical way to approach this if you're looking to have this be the majority of your income. Basically, you don't need to be weird like me, but if you have your own way of going about things there's room for you to do it.

How much can you make as a domme?

You get back what you invest into this. That's a lesson I learn time and time again. That being said, sometimes you can try TOO hard and that backfires. It's not good to invest SO much that it chases away your clients. It's the same as in dating. You want to focus on what you want, you want to be pro-active, but if you lead with wanting it too badly, that comes from a place of desperation which repels.

At the dungeon we were being paid about $200/hr standard, but we also offered certain nude options (more on this later) that made the base rate rise to $280/hr. Depending on whether we were double, triple, etc. domming, our rate was then adjusted. Half of what we made went to the house.

I think a lot of girls think this is easy money, but it's not. To be a good domme it takes skill and smarts. You can coast on your looks for only so long before it starts to work against you. It is the sex industry, and a big part of it is commodifying a woman's body, but, will you be happy if that's all you have to offer?

Being a domme at a dungeon did give me a level of disposable income, but it wasn't what I thought it could be. It's a lot of work per session and a lot of energy. Honestly, all the sacrifices and con-sequences I suffered in my personal life as a result weren't worth the salary I was earning then. I didn't have a financial goal in mind while working at a dungeon so I didn't save. I would advise that if you're going to work at a dungeon, have a financial goal. If you approach it practically and intelligently, you can save a lot of money and build financial security for yourself.

I asked the top earning domme in the dungeon what she was making and she didn't have a clear answer, but I'd guess it was around $8-10k take home pay per month. She was on schedule full time and had 4-5 sessions per day. I was only on schedule 2 or 3 days a week as I had school. On average I was making about 3-5k per month. Holidays tended to be slow as that's family time and subs had difficulty finding alone time to visit the dungeon. Some girls were struggling at the dungeon even if they were on schedule full time so it all depends.

As an independent domme, you set your own rates. Knowing the market is a good idea- most indie dommes make around $250-$500 per hour but just know that if you set your rate high as a beginner, you're most likely not going to be booked very much. If you have regular clients already and have taken time to raise your rates, then a high tribute is more sustainable. You do you. There is absolutely no glass ceiling. Just be realistic and smart. Remember that tribute demarcates a certain "value", at the same time, you want one that feels fair to you. Tribute can also serve as a wall if your rate is extremely high yet you don't have the track record to back it up.

Established dommes will tell you that they don't make that much anymore. Back in the day, dommes were making a boatload. I worked briefly with one woman who dommed more than 10 years ago and made 60k in one month because she was the only Asian domme in the well-established dungeon (back then, and still now overall, Asian dommes are pretty rare), but the industry has changed since. Most dommes now make the bulk of their money from travelling, from clips and from other ventures.

Even though there are more girls in the industry, the greats are few and far between. Many girls see this as a means to an end, meanwhile the ones who really stay and master the craft know that this isn't something you do for money. You have to love it. If you plan on making this your career, you can also teach, run workshops, perform, open a production house for clips, or open up a dungeon depending on where you see yourself and how you want to commit to this. It's great to have a clear goal early on. I unfortunately didn't know what outcome I wanted so I didn't work towards building an infrastructure. If I could do things differently, I'd go back with a goal in mind. That keeps you grounded and centered.

What about findom?

To be a real findom, and not one who posts a picture of a receipt for $10 lunch with "reimburse this paypigs" takes practice and tons of work. It takes building trust, mental and emotional (consensual) manipulation and working hard to maintain that control. I steer clear from findom because it is a tricky territory. Money ALWAYS comes with strings, and if you think that this can just be getting large sums of money to treat someone badly or ignore them, you are gravely mistaken. Surely, you can get lucky and get a real fin-slave who minimizes strings, but in my opinion I would always ask, who's the slave to who? in a real, highly involved financial domination scenario. With findom, the lines are blurry, it verges on personal (what's more personal than money?) and it takes a lot of involvement and energy to do right. I would guess 90% of so called "findoms" aren't real. They just want easy and quick money. I would even categorize findom as edge play because of what money means to so many people and to the world at large.

To me, there's no clearer evidence of power-loss than the fact that findom is a popular activity on sugar daddy dating sites. These sites are set up so that women are at the disadvantage, and men with money are in the power position. That's why there are so many women to men. If findom is popular on here, then who's controlling the strings? Real BDSM in my mind is about real power on the side of the domme, completely surrendered by the sub or slave. In these "findom" scenarios, the domme is usually objectified and a facilitator to something erotic for the "sub"/"slave" who has no interest in truly surrendering, but surrendering in his way and on his terms only and only for his sexual excitement. The penis is in control in these situations. I'm not okay with that.

How do dungeons book for you?

I've seen and heard of many different ways of booking. In my dungeon, we had an administrator who booked for us. We were lucky that we'd only need to come in if we were booked, and we were given a grace period to get ready and travel there if it was a same day booking. Here, we were lucky in that we could blacklist clients we didn't want to see. To have this amount of seeming control is not the standard and of course there was a trade off. They took our liberties in covert ways and played both sides. To keep the dommes, they gave us the illusion of control. To keep their clients, they gave them real control over us.

Most dungeons don't operate this way. I've seen dungeons that needed the girl to book themselves and stay at the dungeon all day when they were on schedule. It looked like this: the girl would put an ad up, then answer and field calls while on site and still split the money with the dungeon owner. That wasn't cool with me- she's doing all the work!

Other dungeons will sometimes have clients come in and choose in person with short interviews. I don't find this particularly cool either because again, the power dynamic isn't in the favor of the domme. But that's the idealist in me. If you work in a place like this you'd have to wait there until a client came in, even if no clients came that day or night.

◆ ◆ ◆

How much can I tell clients about myself?

B ack in the dungeon we were warned about sharing any personal details with a client. I've had many instances where even when I said nothing, clients would find me on social media or dating apps. There will always be cross over no matter how well you hide your foot prints. You need to live your life and that means you'll be visible in some way. It used to freak me out because it was a way a client could leverage power over me when I had more to lose. I've even been threatened before when a sub did his research and found my personal information. Luckily I had nothing to lose then as my family already found out and I was no longer pursuing a career where domming would work against me. The less paranoid you are, the better off you'll be.

I think it's okay to trust your intuition with how much you reveal. So much of this is relationship based, and sometimes to build that connection it's perfectly natural to reveal more as time goes on. The reverse is also true. Sometimes clients compartmentalize and are not looking for real connection in the dungeon. Instead, they want a distant fantasy, someone who they can project their fantasies onto. In those cases, revealing personal details will break the fantasy and make it harder for clients to project onto you. When they're not looking for personal connection and you share information about yourself, they may stop seeing you. Subs who are married generally have less bandwidth in this regard. They may be looking for a safe space where there's no emotional involvement at all.

Use your own judgment and always err on the side of caution. It's never a mistake to take things slower than normal, because if the sub wants to see you, they will. I personally find an overshare to be more damaging than withholding information. A real relationship takes time to build and a massive overshare is a red flag.

Really ask yourself after you start seeing clients what your comfort level is. Look at your own relationships in your real life. Are you closed off and very private, or comfortable being open? See how this does or doesn't translate into your BDSM life. Maybe you're the type of person who leaves work at the office and has a clear separation. Maybe you're the person who stays very connected to their work and clients become friends off the clock. There's no right way to do this but having some sense of non-negotiables is a good idea. Never ever have a personal agenda going into developing a relationship.

Also take into account that because this is more intimate an environment than most people are used to, sometimes re-evaluating and enforcing your boundaries is a great idea. The longer you stay in this industry, the more that happens naturally as a result which can also have an impact on your personal life. Just remain aware and adjust accordingly.

Last note, in the dungeon we were taught to ask a lot of questions and be very chatty with a client. This kind of approach worked well for me then because it does make it a casual, conversational dynamic which can be a refreshing change of pace for some clients. Nowadays, I only ask pointed questions that are necessary for my work. I now don't think it's good to know that much about your client. I feel it's best to preserve some sense of privacy unless your sub willingly shares. The reason for this is because at the dungeon there was already a boundary of the dungeon so clients didn't feel like they were your friend even if you were chatty and casual. When you're independent, there's no barrier and clients can expect you to be both their friend and their domme. **Remember: you're their domme, not their friend, therapist, wife, girlfriend** and it's good to remind them, and yourself, of this. Otherwise, you'll find yourself in a taxing territory that can lead to drain and resentment.

◆ ◆ ◆

How do you prevent burn out?

I n a dungeon it's hard to prevent burn out since you're not the one booking. If you have the flexibility to put less days on the schedule, exercise it. It always helps to give yourself a day off here and there, even if it's hard to say no to money. Trust me, it helps with longevity. When you say no to money because you're honoring yourself, that's when the universe presents more opportunities because you're sending a clear signal that you are autonomous, that you will not sacrifice your own well being for materialism. If you're a slave to money, how can you truly be on the other side of the power exchange?

As an independent, since you're setting your own schedule, just be mindful of when you're exhausted, how many sessions you can comfortably do in a day, in a week, in a month. Set your parameters based on this information and stick to it. Once in a while you can make an exception, but always put you, your health before money or a client's needs. In all cases, taking LESS bookings rather than more will help you feel better in the long run. You'll also be more excited and more eager to session. That enthusiasm goes a long way.

Because I session so infrequently, when I do take a session, I feel so excited. This then fuels my process of getting ready and I bring my whole self into the session. When we're at burn out, what happens is that emotionally and mentally we may be "escaping" in session from the present reality that we're exhausted. This reads as us not being fully "there". Your sub is counting on you to be "there" because that's half the energy exchange. If you're exhausted and not adding any energy, you may be draining your client.

When I am at burn out, my creativity suffers too. My sessions then become repetitive as I go on autopilot. When I have less sessions, I put my all into each hour and find novel and creative ways to do certain things because my mind is invigorated. That's what I found in the dungeon, and as an independent I now know that I can only take 1 session a day max because of what they've become. I know that I max out at half a day, having done all nighters and even all weekend sessions before that took a toll on me. Yes you get a hefty stack of cash from those, but it also took me a long time to recover from them. The time lost recovering my own health was not worth it. When you work in energy, you start to be conscious of putting your energy first. You learn to guard it like a newborn baby because you need energy to get other resources, but money or other resources can never bring back energy.

How does nudity come into play?

I t doesn't typically. The actuality is that in the industry, nudity in session isn't well regarded.

It did for me because I worked at the only dungeon that had their girls photograph and advertise nude. It was the main deal breaker for me initially, and talking to a domme who had been in the industry for a while brought to light that no other dungeon does this. The dungeon I was at was using a porn business model for enticing clients and it's generally seen as a cheap ploy, plus then it attracts the wrong type of client in my opinion. No one expects you to get naked in the session, in fact, most serious dommes stay dressed because the clothing makes an impact in the power dynamic, it serves as a uniform of authority, and it also locks in the CFNM dynamic (clothed female nude male) making the sub feel more submissive when he is naked in front of a dressed domme.

That being said, you can if you want to. That's up to you. I haven't done a nude session since I left the dungeon. I do photograph nude still, but that's not for advertising. It's purely for arts sake and a statement that the female body is beautiful, natural, and we as women don't need to feel ashamed for being naked especially in a sexual assault and sex negative, slut shaming culture. Being comfortably naked makes me feel powerful as a human being, as a woman, but as a domme in session I still prefer to be dressed. It creates a visual boundary too, leaving more to the imagination.

What should I wear in session?

It's good to have a few basics in each category: latex, leather, PVC, lingerie (including garters and stockings) and role-play costumes. My dungeon had a full wardrobe so we never needed our own clothes, but we could incorporate our own if we wanted to. You'll come to find that fetishwear is very expensive so if you don't want to invest initially, just get one or two solid pieces in black so that you can wear them over and over. Repeat clients like to see variety though, so don't rely on this for too long. In my opinion, lingerie is most universal and a leather corset makes any look. It's a good idea to get a custom corset from a specialty store. Latex can get difficult to take care of but it's expected that a domme would have some latex. Out of everything, I think latex is worth the investment. Cheap latex doesn't flatter the body the same way as a nicely tailored piece.

Some established independent dommes wear high end clothing, but you don't need to wear high end clothing to your sessions at all. I like to mix and match some high end, couture items with lower end pieces just to give my outfits more personality. Plus it's more fun for me. When else am I ever going to get the chance to walk around in stripper heels or wear a fishnet leotard? I have plenty of other opportunities to wear expensive heels and outfits though.

Keep in mind that men are visual, that's a biological fact. A lot of BDSM is visually oriented too, and the work itself relies on visuals whether that be in ads or social media. Your clothing can become your signature and although people (depending on what type of clients you have) may ask to see you in certain outfits, it's in your benefit to switch things up as much as possible if you desire to upkeep a high social media profile. I personally don't allow my subs to choose my outfits like the dungeon used to, but I do sometimes consider their fetishes and incorporate them if I so choose. For instance, a heavy latex fetishist or leather fetishist will let you know when they apply because the outfit is the cornerstone of their session.

Sometimes these categories even create a signature. For instance, there are some mistresses who are famous for latex, or other mistresses who are famous for leather. For me, clothing isn't so much my signature. I choose to make people look within, but having great outfits doesn't hurt!

How much gear should I buy?

If you're starting out at a dungeon, you won't need much. Dungeons are usually well equipped unless you want to bring in your own equipment. I would suggest having a few simple items like rope and a flogger to practice at home if you plan on expanding your skills. I didn't own any equipment except for rope when I worked at a dungeon because at such a high sessioning frequency, I used my sessions as practice. Sometimes I utilized the time while we were waiting for our next clients for practice and asked the senior dommes questions.

If you're independent, you also don't need much if you're renting dungeon space because the rentals usually come with equipment rentals too. I opted to buy my own tools because I like feeling prepared and knowing exactly what I have at my disposal. I also like the familiarity of my own implements-- if it's what you practice on, you'll automatically be better at wielding them in session. I feel like I can't consider myself seriously as a domme if I don't have my own tools, not to mention at the beginning of being independent I was available for outcalls so I needed to bring what I had.

If you choose to get your own equipment, you'll come to find it's extremely expensive. You can find some items for cheap on amazon, but they're usually of lower quality. Sometimes you can find good deals and good quality on Etsy and they're often better than ones you can get at sex shops. Some things like floggers, whips and cuffs are worth the investment from specialty shops, because the cheap ones may break skin or break easily. Other things, like butt-plugs for instance, don't matter that much depending on whether you get the $10 one on amazon or the $40+ in store. Sometimes the items are the same, but just bear a higher markup at a sex shop. A lot of times, subs will also bring their own toys or buy you items. At the very beginning of my independent career, I had a sub who took me shopping and bought me a few things to start out with.

A few things that will be helpful to own when starting out are:

Rope (both cotton and hemp- some clients have a preference. Order this on Amazon to start before investing in specialty rope. Make sure it's made for bondage. You won't want to get rope from the hardware store because that can be too harsh on the skin)

Cuffs (these are worth the investment. A good pair of leather cuffs last forever and can withstand all sorts of usage)

Gag (order these on Amazon. Silicone gags are less taxing on the jaw)

Hood

Cane (rattan canes. The thinner the more they sting, so to start it's good to get a medium sized one. Avoid plastic or rubber to start because those hit very hard and will mark unless you're using them on a pain slut with a high pain threshold or someone who wants to be marked)

Flogger (a warm up flogger with thicker, shorter tails is a good place to start. You can't go wrong with those and they're easy to use)

Whip (a signal or a snake whip. For hygiene purposes, a snake whip would be best because the the cracker is removable)

Paddles (Wood or silicone. Avoid plastic ones to start. Those are nasty!)

Candles (made for the body. Also note that white candles burn the most. The darker the color, the less it hurts so choose accordingly)

Blindfold

Various toys (just things to build into your session that can be found at any sex store)

For more advanced kits:
Medical grade sounds & surgical lube (order these on Amazon or through a medical supply store. Only use these if you have proper training)
Needles (order these via medical supply stores)
Leather straps, chains, clips
Sissification clothing (wigs, lingerie, breast cups, shoes)
Tens-unit & attachments (I still don't have this. It's not worth the investment to me as a unit is about $300+. I'm not big on electric play and no one has ever requested this from me since I went independent. Some dungeons will have these on hand even if they say they don't)

And you can go to the hardware store or pharmacies to pick up some basics like:

First aid (it's always a good idea to have a kit on hand. At most dungeons they'll have them)
Gloves
Clothespins
Clamps
"Barriers" (for toys so they stay hygienic)
Ear plugs (for sensory deprivation)
Alcohol pads (for sterilizing in case of needles)
Hydrogen Peroxide (for sterilizing)

A pet store for:

Collars, leashes and cages (They tend to be less expensive than ones made for humans)

Puppy pads

Other things you can assemble yourself like all your old makeup into a sissification kit. Make sure to sterilize these items, however. You may want to consider adding a few random things for games or humiliation. At my dungeon we used to have dice, markers (washable) and finger/hand puppets.

All things silicone can be boiled to clean them. Metal can too, but I've also heard that sometimes this can degrade the metal. If it's something you can't boil, wipe it down with a toy cleaner, soap or hydrogen peroxide and then wash it.

Once you put on BDSM goggles, you'll see potential equipment in every store. To me, it's one of the highlights of this job: seeing what you can incorporate in a devious way in session. Let the fun begin...

◆ ◆ ◆

How much should I plan to invest into this?

A lot. I invest about 60-70% of my income back into this. The more you take this seriously, the higher the investment. For instance, my one latex catsuit cost over $1300. Worn with Louboutins that cost me $1200- that's a lot of money for one outfit. As one photographer told me, the way I look at outfits is the way he looks at camera equipment. This all falls into how you brand yourself and what type of clients you want. If you want to brand yourself as high end, it's necessary to invest money into high end gear and outfits along with time on styling and preparation. Commanding a higher tribute needs to match with the amount of effort. You can't come into this thinking you'll make bank while minimizing your own effort or using cheap toys. You can only get by for so long because it's noticeable and will work against you.

You don't have to be like me and invest THAT much back into your work. I'm thinking long long term so that's why it makes sense to me now. I used to play it safe when I wasn't sure of my trajectory, but I also came to realize that sometimes you do need to go "balls to the wall" because production value shows.

Beyond fiscal investment, my work takes a lot of emotional, mental and physical investment. This can be an emotionally taxing space. A lot of mistresses can and do feel drained because of the level of responsibility and the co-dependent structures we're working within. Not to mention, this territory is naturally emotional even if there are boundaries and dynamics in place. I care a lot about my clients, so that too is an emotional investment.

This can be a physically demanding job, so be prepared. Sometimes after a session with corporal play, my arms and wrists are sore for days. You're often times handling the body weight of a grown man especially if you get involved in advanced techniques like suspension. Also, consider that you're running the session and engaging in physically demanding activities in heels so sometimes your legs will hurt.

◆ ◆ ◆

What are clients like?

C lients are so different. They range from the classic leader who needs an outlet to let go of the pressure of responsibility to the lifestyle sub who has markings on him from all the mistresses he's had in his life. Some are trying this out for novelty, some are seasoned. Some understand protocols, some don't, and some are disrespectful on purpose. Some have deep unresolved traumas they don't want to heal but rather project onto you, others are drawn to the resolution that BDSM and the right mistress can offer. Most of them, you'd never guess would be a sub if you met them on the street.

Some struggle with shame for what they're into because the rest of their lives are so conservative. Other people live very openly and share that they're with a domme with their partner. Some are as young as 18 and some are well into their 70's. There's no constant, except that most of them tend to be Caucasian and have disposable income.

At my dungeon, the protocol was for the sub to get undressed in a mud room prior to entering the playroom. As the domme, you'd walk through the mud room first before greeting the sub in the playroom. I used to love guessing what the person was like and what career they had, upon seeing their folded clothes and catching the scent of their cologne. It also was an interesting thought to know that I was their secret that day, one that only he and I knew about.

Now, I would say for the most part I've noticed that the men I see are all very stressed out and burdened by their lives in some way. They need a place where they can deeply surrender and gain perspective, not to mention their energy is usually blocked up. A lot of men often shut down through life, because our culture is geared towards men repressing their emotions and seeming "strong" in a way that breaks down their connection to self, feeling and flow. They then close up and shut down.

You'll come to see that even though everyone's varied, and that you're bound to come across one or two surprises along the way, for the most part everyone seems knew they were kinky since they were very, very young.

Do I need a website?

If you work through a dungeon, you'll be listed on their website and many dungeons have non-competes, so you aren't allowed to make a separate website or social media. If you're independent, you definitely need a website. The content can be sparse, but you at least want to have somewhere for clients to land and a way for them to contact you.

I first used wordpress to create my website because I wanted it to be blog focused. My former dungeon had a forum linked to their website, and that's where I had the most draw because I wrote a lot about my discoveries in BDSM. I knew that my writing was where I could most clearly express myself and my complex ideas about identities, BDSM and life, so I wanted to show that side of myself in my independent work too.

I later came to feel stifled by the templates. It looked unprofessional and I couldn't program it the way I wanted so I migrated over to squarespace. Although you can't have a web store as a sex worker on squarespace (mine got shut down several times), the rest of it is seamless and it takes a minimal amount of effort to design it since the templates are all so beautiful already. My advice for designing a website: make it clean and visually focused. Imagine that your viewer has only 5 minutes and you need to direct him/her/them to exactly what s/he/they need to know and see. Too much clutter overwhelms. It's okay to have many pages, but make sure the navigation is organized. Squarespace websites are mobile-optimized. If you choose a different service or work with a designer, make sure they do this for you. Most of my audience looks at my site on their phone.

It's a good idea to list your interests and limits on the page so clients that apply to see you already know if it matches theirs. That will save you a lot of time in the long run because you won't have to explain them over email or in person.

◆ ◆ ◆

Do I need business cards?

Not really. I have them and have distributed them in the past, but the likelihood of a potential client holding onto a card is slim. Think about it- these people need utmost privacy regarding their interest in BDSM, that's why most will even have a separate anonymous email account called something like: "submissivesissyboy@gmail.com". If they're married and their wives catch them with concrete evidence like a business card, what would that do?

The likelihood of it being tossed in the garbage is higher than the likelihood of it being kept in most cases.

That being said, it's fun designing a card, and you can pick and choose who to give it to. In the past I've left some of mine at sex shops. The have no tangible evidence of success, as no one's ever mentioned they found my business card. In the entirety, I haven't found business cards to be entirely fruitful, more annoying when I accidentally have them laying around and the dog sitter or house cleaner sees them, but it can't hurt to have more collateral.

◆ ◆ ◆

Do I need a business line?

Y es you do. You don't want to use your real phone number. Most girls use google voice. It's a free service and I've found that it's very private and secure, not to mention you can toggle your line on and off so that your phone isn't ringing all through the night.

You can also use a burner phone, or the burner phone app. In my opinion, google voice is less sketchy. You don't want to keep changing your phone number because that will throw people off. If you keep only one thing constant in your whole business, make it the way they contact you.

Some clients who I become close with have my real number, and my old personal subs had it too, so I'm not saying that you can't share that. It's just ill-advised to use it with the general public. You don't want people to have direct access to you for many security reasons because some people will opt to abuse it.

◆ ◆ ◆

Where do I advertise?

M ost girls advertise on eros.com, even though it's getting sketchier and sketchier. You can't even contact them directly anymore, and changes to your ads take a while to approve. Be aware that if you're advertising here you'll need to upload a photo of yourself and your ID. I've purchased upgrades that haven't run which is a total waste, and once in a while they'll charge you random service fees that they hope you don't notice.

There's no way to get these refunded because you can't contact them.

I rarely advertise anymore, as most of my traffic comes through instagram or google. Surprisingly, most of my applicants are people who have known about me and read my blog for months before they contact me so I'm not even sure that advertising is that successful for me.

There are some femdom directories online that other mistresses have had success with (Dickie Virgin, etc), some websites like hogspy advertise travel for free for a specific audience. You can also buy an ad to be featured on the page for a month at a time, but I don't use those services anymore.

Most other methods of advertising like backpage are gone. Those types of ads typically are lower end and more immediate. Although I didn't use backpage, when I asked other dommes, they said that they've gotten good clients off of it. My old dungeon used to advertise on backpage and the majority of their clients came from there. I've witnessed the process at a dungeon that asked girls to book themselves: the girls would post an ad on backpage with a few photos (the dungeon owner said upskirt shots do the best) and calls would come in immediately. I write this just in case there's another service like backpage in the future so you know what to expect. Most higher end practitioners advertise on eros but as that's fading away, I'm not sure what the next reputable place is.

Some rating sites like TER I would recommend you avoid. You can advertise on TER and my old dungeon required that we have one, but it's for hobbyists who objectify and demean girls and rate them based on their breasts, how they groom their pubic hair and performance etc..

I like to keep a low profile mostly as I do believe that the people who are meant to find you will. But most dommes who want higher volume will advertise on google and get their google ranking up and set up multiple websites. I've tried this before and it got so expensive with little payoff. It wasn't worth it to me.

◆ ◆ ◆

What kind of email account should I use?

I've had a gmail account since the beginning of my indie career and that's my preferred method. Most of what I do isn't "in the dark" because I ask for my client's verifiable full name. The people who come to me have to be comfortable with disclosing a lot of information with me which tends to attract a more open sub. Many girls don't book like this, and for people who have clients who need much more discretion, it's good to get an email that is encrypted.

Protonmail is encrypted, and if you get .ch instead of .com, that's even more secure apparently. For phone interviews, whats app is encrypted. Just make sure that it's not linked to your real name.

◆ ◆ ◆

Should I offer a consultation?

Y es you should have this as an option and make sure it's in public and paid. Sometimes if it's not an in-person consultation, I'll take one on niteflirt so that my time and energy are being compensated. If you set this parameter, then you tend to have more serious subs. In my consultations I usually offer a healing too but that's not necessary. You're there to answer questions, get a feel for your potential sub's background, and then you both decide whether a session feels right.

Consultations I feel are for more "on-the fence" situations. Some dommes even allow consultations in the case the sub doesn't want to send in references or ID. I personally don't skip a vetting protocol for a consultation. In addition, I find that a consultation sets a casual tone immediately because there isn't a power dynamic in public. Clients tend to use this time to confide in you and unless you're building trust and rapport through a detailed intake, this can sometimes be draining. Unless you're building a long term relationship, all that information is unnecessary.

I used to struggle with boundaries in these situations as they felt so personal. But make sure you set them. After an hour you're not required to be there even if your potential client has more to talk about. Your time is valuable and you do not owe emotional labor or time.

With consultations, I would say that only a small percentage were people I ended up sessioning with. The reason being, if they were already committed to sessioning they would apply for a session. In the times I've offered a consultation, I'm leading with the feeling that a session doesn't feel right so I'm taking more time to decide. My gut instinct is almost always right and I reach the conclusion that it's a no-go. Most times when someone is applying for a consultation they're just wanting an ear anyway.

Can I do this alone?

Yes you certainly can. I used to have a few friends in the industry but over the years have decided to operate solo. As a lone wolf type, being independent is great for me because I'm not beholden to anyone and can do what I want when I want. This is your business and you can lead it your way. There's a great community in New York where I'm based so if you're extroverted and love networking, there are so many wonderful people to meet and work with.

Being alone doesn't hurt my business because of the way it's set up. In mine, I don't do multi-domme sessions. For those of you who want to do multi-domme sessions, then definitely socialize, join collectives if they resonate, go to parties, reach out to other dommes and see if they're open to meeting one on one.

The companionship is part of the reason some girls may choose to stay at the dungeon. If you're more social and extroverted, it can feel great being around other dommes. So pick and choose based on your personality.

At the beginning of my indie career, I had a few women who knew what I was doing and were involved in the industry. That helped me feel more secure as I figured out how to vet, how to book, how to trust my intuition. I used to tell one of my friends where I was going as a security measure and we had a check in process. As I got to the door, I'd tell her along with the length of the session. I'd text her again after I met the client and was changing in the bathroom so she knew that the guy was fine. If she didn't hear back from me in a certain time frame, she'd know to contact authorities (this never happened luckily). That protocol died out early on because it became unnecessary. My safety is not a risk anymore as it used to be when I had less knowledge and control. I would recommend you have at least 1 friend, even if she/he/they isn't/aren't in the industry, who knows what you're doing so that she/he/they can become your emergency contact just in case things go wrong.

◆ ◆ ◆

What can we write in our emails and discuss with our clients?

With anything written and therefore permanent, stay as vague as possible. Do not confirm activities and do not discuss anything illegal. If clients push, tell them you'll discuss it with them during your negotiation.

Back in the dungeon, even in-person we weren't allowed to say certain words. In email communications, intake had a whole list of abbreviations so never were any activities written out.

Make sure to check your state's laws regarding what is deemed "prostitution". It's better in this regard to be safe than sorry.

◆ ◆ ◆

Do I answer my emails as a domme?

Y ou can definitely email as a domme so you establish that rapport immediately. It's also fun to be able to do that. Back in the day I used to answer my emails as a domme and was very demanding, but as I've grown it becomes less important for me to "play" a domme. I've grown more confident, gotten better with boundaries and communication that I am just me. If you think that comes across dominant, fine. If not, also fine.

This is a personal choice and it doesn't hurt to experiment.

◆ ◆ ◆

What do I do with disrespectful clients over email?

A lot of subs will try to push your boundaries from the get go through email. They may email you repetitively with no regard for your time. They'll ask all sorts of nonsense things and email you like they're texting you just to try to keep the conversation going. I used to get mad and tell them to stop, but sometimes they're baiting you to do that so if you give them that kind of attention they'll keep going.

My advice: BLOCK. It's not worth your time or energy. People like them are a dime a dozen and you won't lose a potential client because most of these people are time wasters and won't actually book with you.

Also watch out for people who try to leverage money to bait your time. For instance, they'll talk about financial domination and how much money they want to give you without actually doing it. In these situations just ignore, or make them prove to you they're serious. They're engaging in a covert powerplay here and trying to establish their dominance. It comes from a sense of entitlement: "I have money so I have control,"

◆ ◆ ◆

How do we keep ourselves safe and within the law?

V et carefully! I've never had encounters with law enforcement or busts, but I have heard that they will ask a lot of questions about what services you perform at the get-go so as to build a case. If you feel a strange feeling, or notice that your client seems particularly nosey, stop responding. It's not worth it. There are a lot of people who will tell you that cops don't waste time busting dommes- what's the point? But I have heard of several busts in hotel rooms, even in situations when there was nothing resembling sexual activity.

It may be good to have a criminal defense lawyer that you establish a relationship. Have his/her cards on hand just in case. You'll want to hand this to the cop if s/he asks you any questions. Tell them to talk to your lawyer and answer nothing.

If you do outcalls, make sure the locations aren't sketchy. When I first started I stupidly did outcalls in people's homes (but limited to certain areas in Manhattan). I would never do that again unless it was someone I knew well. All the hotels I went to were at least 4-stars. Now, to keep myself in my comfort zone, I only session at certain dungeons. When other people are around, it keeps you safer. Never session with someone alone in your own home.

Make sure your website and ads allude to no sexual services. It's good to put a disclaimer that you don't offer any illegal activities and stick to that in session.

Make sure that when you're sessioning that you're sober. Make sure that your clients aren't on drugs or prescription medication that can put them at risk. Even if your client took viagra (which some of them may do just to prove a point) for instance, that can make them more likely to faint in certain positions because of how it distributes the blood in the body. Make sure you wear gloves if you're doing any edge play or anything that may expose you to blood. Make sure all of your equipment is clean so that you don't put anyone at risk of infection.

With edge play, make sure you are trained and know what you are doing before performing anything of higher risk. Especially when this territory involves someone's anatomy, establish a clear understanding first. A lot can go wrong, safety wise and you don't want it to fall on you.

Don't leave marks on clients if they say no marks. Don't leave traces of makeup on them if you sissified or feminized them, and don't wear heavy perfumes that may rub off on your clients if you know they have privacy concerns. You don't want their wives thinking they're having an affair. The less trace you leave, the better UNLESS your sub or slave actually wants you to leave marks.

Some subs/slaves have fantasies involving blackmail, or you destroying his/her primary relationship in some way. BE CAREFUL about these situations. Most times, the fantasies themselves are erotic for the sub but the real thing can get out of hand and pin you as the bad guy.

How do I vet clients?

When I verify clients, I ask for full name along with ID, linkedin or if they won't share that information, I ask for 1 or 2 references. With references, make sure they're real, established practitioners. Sometimes subs will list fake references and say that they're "under the radar" or lifestyle dommes. Really, the sub themselves are answering the email as a domme or creating a strange fantasy where you talk to the domme about themselves as third person. Yes, this happens.

With their full name, you can do a google search or look on Facebook to verify their identity.

With just their email, you can use sites like verifyhim.com to see their history and read reviews. If someone has been blacklisted on this site, trust it and stop responding. I've heard some horror stories that have happened to women in the industry because they didn't vet well enough. After the fact, one woman I knew looked the guy up on verifyhim and saw he was blacklisted multiple times.

If the client supplies references, make sure to check them even if they've sent through their ID. I made the mistake once of not checking references once with one of my first independent clients because he had supplied a linkedin and social media links, not to mention had a very well written and thoughtful application. Huge mistake. Luckily nothing terrible happened, but I did find out that he was in law enforcement and had a fake linkedin because of that. Later when I checked his lengthy list of references, most of the women hadn't seen him before, and the ones who did had no idea that he was law enforcement. Sometimes there are cops who want to partake in sessioning for their own pleasure and not because of anything to do with their profession, meaning, they're not trying to bust you. I've never had one of these situations, but if you do, I'm sure they'll be more upfront than anything.

There was also another time when a sub didn't pay me what he owed, which was more than $1000. I trusted him to take care of the payment, which he did prior, but with transferring money online you can mostly always cancel it after. Because he'd passed a few check points and was so incredibly nice during the session, even gifting me nice lingerie, I thought it was just a mistake. Later when I didn't hear back, I checked in with all of his references and no one had a record of him. In both of these cases, the subs had studied the territory well and listed very reputable dommes. It bypassed my better judgment because I thought, if they had this much experience in the industry, knew exactly how to approach me, seemed "well-trained" and respectful, then surely they were for real.

With references, most women in the industry know to respond. It's part of the "code" so to speak. With that said, you need to provide references too. Some dommes prefer that the sub asks first before being listed as a reference. Other times, subs won't ask but will list you anyway. Sometimes, subs who have never seen you before will list you. Other times, subs who have acted uncool towards you will also list you especially if you start to gain a good reputation because again, listing reputable dommes is an easy way to bypass someone's verification process. Be honest with your feedback as it could save someone's life or at the very least, save someone else some trouble. You'd want the same for you.

◆ ◆ ◆

What else should I be vetting for?

I have a submission form on my website that takes into account a lot of the background information besides basic stats. I ask for their experience, what they're interested in and what their limits are. You'd be surprised how much people will disclose sometimes!

The reason I ask for more information than usual is because I care about the psychology of the person. The form helps me build a preliminary understanding in case this is someone I take as a sub. What more is, the more information provided, the more I can get a sense of what type of submissive they are from their tone, their choice of words and their overall vibe.

I look for subs who demonstrate submission. I make my application protocol difficult for a reason— subs need to demonstrate they pay attention to detail and instruction because that's already demonstrating respect and submission. Sometimes if they're booking a consultation I may test them and tell them to bring something or order a drink for me in a specific way.

If a sub automatically approaches me as an equal or that they're better than me, that's a red flag. When someone approaches me as an equal, I'll take it more into consideration depending on other aspects of the form than if they're already topping me. I look for what they're interested in about me as well. If it's purely physical and seems to only be for satisfying their sexual needs, I don't waste another minute because it's wrong for me. My sessions ride on a deeper connection and are healing based.

Most important is the overall feeling. Even if you're not a professional intuitive like me and aren't energy sensitive, your subconscious is already picking up on the vibe of the person. If something feels off and you don't have any evidence, chances are you're probably right regardless.

My sessions have lessened over the years. I take very, very few subs so I am much more stringent with my vetting. Most people though, aren't as strict as I am and I'm sure they meet lots of great people that way that I would've written off. It's up to you how you want to vet and what you want to vet for. I'd say as general advice that you do set certain restrictions like, someone can only call you between certain hours, or you limit how long you spend on the phone, or you ask for certain information via webform otherwise you could be answering calls and emails all day! That's a huge energy drain and not a smart way to streamline your intake process.

Also note- if you do book by phone, be aware that many people will try to take advantage of phone time without serious plans to book with you. They want phone sex and you can tell because they'll sound turned on (heavy breathing) and keep asking questions for detail to get you to describe what you'd do to them. Cut these phone calls short immediately.

Also be vetting for sanity. If someone gives you a reason to believe they are mentally ill, do not take them. There are enough horror stories out there about subs and slaves who commit suicide and then it is blamed on the mistress. If you are an empath like me, you may be drawn to help people who seem ill. But **remember, you cannot fix anyone.**

Good questions to generally ask yourself are: is this person doing what I ask them (within reason) to do, are they wasting my time, and are they showing signs of being challenging? If they already are being difficult because many subs like to test someone's authority, imagine how difficult they're going to be in person.

If they're testing you, remember that in BDSM negative enforcement is sometimes positive reinforcement. Meaning, think about the basic scenario of someone wanting pain as punishment in a session. They want the punishment so they will do the "wrong" thing to get it. Sometimes, subs want to be ignored, humiliated, screamed at and will push you purposely to get that. In these cases, give them the opposite. Be super nice to them and that will chase them away :)

◆ ◆ ◆

How do I handle money?

At the dungeon, cash was taken from the sub during the negotiation and dropped off in the office. It was then distributed to us on our individual lockers. With all sex work, the protocol is to handle money first.

There are several options. You can accept tributes via paypal (make sure it's a business account, not a personal!). I used to take deposits on giftrocket, but because one time I accepted a full tribute on giftrocket and it was later rescinded, I wouldn't suggest this.

Giftrocket and other money transfer apps like square or circle flag large sums of money. Square cash will ban your account if they find out you're a sexworker, and giftrocket won't process amounts like $500+ unless they get a double confirmation by email a few days after the money is sent. In the past, a few people haven't confirmed whether on purpose or because it went to their spam mail.

I've found that accepting a deposit first through paypal or giftrocket is a good way to go to make sure that your time is being compensated even if someone cancels. It also means that someone is serious and isn't a time-waster. The rest can be handled in cash at the time of the session. It's no longer necessary for me to receive cash upfront and I don't count it there because I trust my subs, but in the dungeon we did count it while the client was still there.

To make a business paypal account, you should have an LLC first. If you're pursuing this job seriously, it's best to have an LLC because there are many benefits to having a small business. I like to use paypal because it's more transparent and easier to keep a record of for tax reasons. That being said, note that my sessions are no longer traditional nor strictly BDSM. When they were, I used only giftrocket. Now that they're healing, I use paypal. I have read that paypal shuts down sex worker accounts without warning. If that happens, you won't be able to retrieve your money.

I also know that you can cancel payments on paypal. DO NOT use a personal account because then clients get so much information about you! With a business account, only the name of your business is shown. Note however, that paypal takes a small percentage of larger amounts.

◆ ◆ ◆

Should I account for the dungeon rental fee in my tribute?

Some girls do and some girls don't. I factor it into my rental fee, and for some time when I first started because I set my business up to be outcall only, when clients booked an incall the rental fee would be covered by them. When clients booked hotel rooms, they knew to cover that fee.

There are so many ways to do this. A lot of women don't build in the rental fee, keeping it the same for out and incall, and it is then deducted from their tribute.

Dungeons in New York and LA are usually $80/hr. To book a dungeon space you'll usually meet with the owner if it's privately owned and then you let them know ahead of time for bookings. You usually pay them after the session is done. Some are lenient about cancellations or no-shows because in this industry, for most people the bookings move fast and are last minute. I would advise you to have a cancellation policy that you enforce so that if someone cancels or makes changes within the window, you can book someone else.

I have a strict cancellation policy and I usually know of my sessions weeks in advance. In my independent career I've had 0 no-shows. I know this is very, very rare. It all depends on your priorities and your business model.

If you're just starting out, never invite your clients into your personal space unless it's a shared dungeon space and other people are around. It may be tempting to session from home because there's no overhead, but don't. I recently heard a horror story about a domme who started seeing her regulars in her own home. One of them she'd known for years turned on her and robbed her. You never know what triggers some people have even if you've known them for years. You're only seeing them in confined spaces that may not be reflective of the totality of who they are.

Do I need photos?

Yes you absolutely do. Even if you keep a low profile, you need a few photos (5-10 good ones) to advertise with and to have on your website. Most women have a gallery on their website and some even have subscription services like onlyfans.com or patreon.com where they release exclusive photos for a monthly subscription fee.

At the time of writing this, I only just subscribed to onlyfans. For a long time I was against selling photos, but because of the large amount of investment I was making in my photos, I knew that I needed to be paid a little to supplement the effort, time and money. The format of onlyfans appeals to me more than patreon because it's like social media. Patreon in my opinion, demands more time because you set up rewards per month for your subscribers and release full photo sets at a time.

If you work for a dungeon, they'll arrange photoshoots for you and update them when they can. It's in their favor to have current photos because the worst thing that can happen is if a client books a mistress and sees that he was catfished. In my old dungeon when things were running smoothly we shot every few months.

If you are independent, one of the first steps before you start officially working is to book a photographer. I would recommend your first shoot not be an artistic collaboration, as in, pay a professional who has experience with shooting ads. Since you're starting out, you may have little experience to know which shots would be best for you. You want little to no room for error during your first shoot as this is the gateway to working.

For my first shoot, I hired a photographer who shot my friend after I saw her ad photos. I booked a hotel room and bought several outfits. Although I felt more comfortable doing my own hair, makeup, styling, you may want to invest in those too. Remember these aren't just photos, they're what's going to get you work so it's worth the investment.

From that point on, I began collaborating with photographers on photos for my social media and website. These were more artistic and the photographers are not shooting what they feel would work well on ads, they're purely shooting in their style which makes a huge difference. Depending on their background, they want photos that work in fashion or art which are not at all the same as what does well in ads. After you have a few solid photos for advertising, then you can get creative with your other content as it always helps to have fresh content to keep interest.

In the sex industry, a huge discovery was that selfies work best. It's good to throw in a selfie here and there alongside professional photos because they're more accessible. Clients know that if you took a selfie, you really look like that and they feel closer to you.

This is the same thing that applies on social media. The percentage I've come to find is that 1/3 of the highest views and likes go to professional photos, and 2/3 goes to selfies, or candid photos take on a phone. Don't, however, make all of your photos selfies. That can come off lazy or that you're not serious about what you do. When people hire a professional, they want a professional so mix polished media with some fun low-key ones. People want to know you're a well-rounded, real person who takes their job seriously.

What do I wear in my advertisement photos, how should I do my hair/makeup?

V ariety is key. Surprise is key. But what's more key is feeling and looking good.

You want to accentuate your curves and wear something you feel sexy in. If you feel uncomfortable, it's going to show in the photos.

For a first shoot, I'd pick 3-4 outfits for a 3 hour shoot. I'd pick a lingerie set complete with stockings, a latex outfit, and a harder outfit like leather. If you're just starting out it's good to verge on more classic attire and then take more risks as time goes on. You're setting your foundation here not just with your image, but with building your wardrobe, so it's better to stick with the tried and true.

I usually do my own hair and makeup. Reason being, I am used to the way I do it and that means I feel more comfortable when I shoot. There have been times when a professional has done my hair and makeup and it feels strange. I don't feel attractive and that translates to awkward photos. There has also been a time when a professional hair stylist chopped off 4 or more inches of my hair when she asked if she could trim less than an inch off, while she was styling it for a shoot. After that I've been reluctant to let anyone style it. Once in a while I'll get my hair blown out for a shoot for a more polished look. That never hurts.

Make sure to put some effort into this. I cannot reiterate enough how big of a part of your business photos are. If you look like you put no effort into it and are wearing yesterday's makeup, no one's going to take you seriously unless that slept-in look is their fetish.

I personally like my makeup on the light side. I don't even wear foundation. But remember, professional lighting is going to wash out a lot of the color, so it's not a bad idea to put on a little more blush or eyeshadow than usual. Back in the dungeon, the headmistress made us coat on our blush and bronzer. I remember being told during my first photoshoot that I had to keep applying blush, bronzer and powder 4 times. I felt like my face looked striped like a zebra. We also weren't allowed to wear red lipstick and we had to make our eyes very smokey. That's one aesthetic, but I can say from experience that caking on makeup like that will make you look old. My clients then would come into session and say, "wow you look nothing like your photos," or, "you look so much younger and better in person," which is more or less what the dungeon wanted. News would spread on the dungeon forum that I looked better in person, piquing curiosity from other potential clients. It's better to look better in person than worse, but not drastically different.

Although I wear red lipstick sometimes and significantly lessen my makeup, the smokey eye look has stuck with me. I do tend to wear more eyeliner in my shoots than in every day. It makes my eyes more intense and I look less innocent and sweet. In photos, I don't think clients are looking for what you look like every day. You may not even want to look that approachable unless you're sure that your branding is "the girl next door" or something similar. They want to see you how you'd look in their fantasy.

I don't think that the place for radical experimentation with makeup or hair is here. For artistic photoshoots, certainly, especially after people are used to what you look like and recognize your face. For the purposes of advertisements, keep with the intention to highlight your sexiness and beauty. A little "blankness" is okay, because that's easier to project a fantasy on. From there, whether you want to look more feminine, more harsh, more intimidating, more youthful is completely up to you.

Remember that there's no reason to be self-conscious. You don't need to be a professional model to take good photos.

What happens if you have a bad experience with a photographer?

I believe that most women who shoot regularly will have at least one bad experience with a photographer. There are many creepy photographers out there who try to bait women in sex work because it's a turn on for them, not to mention, on photoshoots, the power usually is with the photographer most of the time since he/she/they is/are directing it and have control over the camera, what photos to send, when to send them.

A lot of weird control games happen here. Some of them are very subtle, like withholding. Sometimes, it can be confusing especially when a photographer seems nice but there's still uncool behavior. For instance, they may try to convince you to do certain uncomfortable things, or they're hitting on you in a creepy way, or getting sexually excited. Some photographers may try to take advantage of you, like attempting to get you to do certain session activities with them so that they can "shoot it" but really, they're trying to get a free session out of you. Sometimes after the shoot, they continue to cling onto you and cross lines by trying to convince you to play or do shoots that are mirroring their fetish. If you intuitively sense that the collaboration itself isn't so much important to them as what they can get from you out of it, like time, attention, sexual favors, then flag this and know never to work with this person again.

Sometimes they can be a cool person, but want to get to know you in ways that are invasive, or they expect you to be their therapist or help them figure out their kinks. Not your job. You're there to shoot. If there's a friendly rapport, then of course you can be friends with your photographer. You're not there, however, to do anything else nor do you owe anything else.

Initially, I wasn't sure what the difference was between being objectified in a sexual way by a photographer and taking explicit photos for the sake of the photos themselves. I've never had harmful situations, but I have had uncomfortable situations when my own boundaries weren't so clear. It came from spending a lot of time in a dungeon where I got used to being sexually objectified. I walked into any situation as a "domme" subconsciously thinking it was my job to turn the other person on.

With experience, I learned what was a respectful photoshoot. The dynamic should be feel nice and even. The photographer cares about how you're shot and whether you're happy with the photos. There's a good give and take- some photos s/he may use for his/her own portfolio, and you have photos that you like that you can use either on your social media, website or ads. It should never feel like it's done for the service of someone over the other unless it's negotiated that way, or someone is being paid. A good trade is one that feels healthy and balanced. You don't owe anything to them and they don't owe you anything either.

Many photographers will ask you to sign a release form so that they can use the images. Just make sure to review the whole form and see what rights you're signing away. Sometimes, if the photographer is savvy and seasoned, it can be written to benefit them a lot more than you (i.e. they can sell the photos and not give you a cut).

In situations when the photographer holds too much control, I've often felt disappointed in the photos. Yes, they can be very experienced and have a certain aesthetic, or way they see you and think you photograph best, but usually in those situations they aren't being true to who I really am. It's their vision, I'm just a prop. Be wary of photographers who want you to work on their journalistic project about dommes and find out who else they've shot before you agree. Talk to them on the phone and ask what they're aiming to capture. See if that's in line with your ethos. Sometimes it can be completely off-brand and may be making a statement that you're not comfortable with.

Make sure that they know they can't use a photo unless it's approved by you first. Make sure you mutually agree on submissions to magazines. This is your image and these decisions need to be run by you unless you sign away your rights. It's okay to be explicit about your boundaries right off the bat. I've found that it helps if people know what you will and won't do beforehand, so no one wastes time. This too is a good way to practice your negotiation skills.

◆ ◆ ◆

Should I watermark my images?

Some dommes do and some dommes don't. Anything you put out there means that anyone can take it- I can't even tell you how many fake accounts I've heard of on all sorts of dating sites or apps. Some people have even reported a fake me in Beijing named "Claire".

I choose not to watermark most of my images, because watermarks look so ugly. No matter what, people are going to steal your images. Even if you have a watermark on your face in a photo, someone's going to photoshop that out if they really want to take your image. It's unavoidable. Unless you want to copyright every single one and go after every person who uses an image of yours, just relax. This is the internet age. If you don't want anyone to use any images, then don't distribute them. But then, what's the fun in that?

The bigger your profile becomes, the more people will use your images. However, the bigger your profile becomes, the more people will know who those images are of. The interesting thing is, you may think that putting up a sloppy selfie would get the least amount of attention or people stealing it, but it's actually those that get stolen the most.

If you choose to watermark your images, there are so many apps that make that quick and efficient. Or you can always use photo-shop.

Should I blur my face?

I would say no. Blurring your face instills a certain sense of shame, of hiding. A lot of sex workers do blur their face though if it can compromise them to be "found out". This is a personal choice- if you have a lot to lose, have plans for a van-illa career, or currently have a job in an industry where domming could be costly, then maybe it's the right choice for you.

My stance is that if being a domme is going to be so risky in your life to the point you need to blur out your face, then it might not be the best life choice for you. If you're blurring your face because you find domming shameful, again, maybe not the best choice to domme I took domming as an opportunity to work through my shame, not towards it.

Which photos should I use to advertise?

A s I mentioned before, selfies do well. Plan to have 3-4 solid professional shots and one or two selfies taken in dungeons.

It can help to have photos with a slave or sub in them, because then it gives potential clients the opportunity to project themselves into the photos and feel closer to you. It triggers, "I want to be him!" along with the possibility that this fantasy can be real since they see it. However, it's not necessary. I don't typically shoot with a sub because I want to preserve the intimate space of me alone, with the viewer.

I've found that photos with direct eye contact do better than photos where there isn't, because it establishes a connection.

Try to pick shots where the angle is either face level or from below you so you look tall and domineering. Try not to use photos where the camera is shooting from above you unless it's an artistic shoot. That indicates subservience and can make you look small.

Should I use networking sites like fetlife, collarspace or whiplr?

Y ou can definitely. I've gotten clients on collarspace when I was on it years ago. Make sure if you're using it purely professionally to indicate that on all your profiles because on any of these networking sites, you'll mostly get lots of people who want to be your friend or play with you in a personal context. If your intention isn't clear, you're going to attract people who aren't clear on your boundaries either.

Fetlife, in my experience, is great for finding personal subs. I don't use it much anymore because unless you get lucky, it can prove to be taxing to sort through all the applications and set up interviews etc.. But I have heard of many other dommes who have had great experiences finding errand boys, cleaning boys, chauffeurs, service subs, etc. From my experience, I'd rather pay someone to do these activities for me because it simplifies everything and you're getting professional level service. I know there are many mistresses who would disagree with me. I rarely take personal service oriented subs because with anything not mediated by money, there are strings.

If you want to experiment with your kink life, any of these sites are a great way to go. However, be aware that it can be very hit or miss and trust your judgment.

You have nothing to lose by making a profile as it can serve as free advertising to get your name out there. I personally had no luck on whiplr, but go right ahead! My experience isn't everyone's.

◆ ◆ ◆

Should I get on social media?

In this day and age, I say yes, that is, if you don't mind visibility. Although I don't get BDSM clients off social media, it does serve as a way to allow people to follow and get to know you. It keeps their interest and builds a persona. I would aim to post a few times a week. Solid professional shots do well as actual posts. Selfies are great once in a while as posts but do extraordinarily well in stories. Reveal a little of what you do when you're not domming. It helps to keep the audience engaged when you show you have other interests, are a real person and aren't just playing a part.

Social media is a self-promotional tool. If you're someone who'd rather be low-key and privacy is a concern for you, then it's best not to make accounts. Most indie dommes have social media accounts. It's become a necessity for entrepreneurs.

◆ ◆ ◆

How do I set my own limits?

I recommend figuring out what you're willing to do and what you're not willing to do before you enter the industry. For instance, I knew immediately that I wouldn't offer brown or red showers. At the dungeon, other girls had other limits, like no coddling sessions, simply because it annoyed them. It's all based on individual preferences. You don't have to do everything and you most of all won't want to do anything you hate even if it could make you money.

You should also have a working knowledge of your own boundaries. For instance, how much bodily contact is okay for you? How much skin will you show? What types of worship will you allow? Many subs will come into this wanting to make the session as sexual as possible, so it helps if you already know where you aren't willing to go. Make sure they know too, because I've heard of some subs assuming one thing meant something else. There are subs who also want to build a long term relationship because they think that as time goes by you'll loosen your boundaries and allow more sexual things that you once said no to. They may have had this in the past so they think it's perfectly reasonable. If you sense this is the case, it's best to ask them directly what their motives are so that you establish at the get go you won't allow this. That way there aren't invisible strings you're beholden to and no one feels deceived.

Other limits develop over time as you get to know your preferences. What you might've thought you were fine with may turn into something you don't want to engage in later. You can adjust your limits as you go, you're never locked into anything.

A disclaimer here: there are a few fetish activities that not everyone offers, including scat play or real cuckholding scenarios. For various reasons, these are on most people's limits list. If you do decide you're willing to offer these, then it can become your specialty and you can charge a premium for them.

It's a good idea to let your clients know before sessioning for the first time what you won't offer just so they know not to expect those activities. This is important especially if they're asking for something that can sit in a gray area. For instance, if they want "smothering" or "breath play" it's a good idea to establish that you will smother them with your hand or another part of your body you're comfortable with but that doesn't mean that you will "face sit" or expose them to any intimate body parts. As you start feeling more comfortable controlling the session, however, it will be a complete nonissue because the session already happens within your limits and boundaries. The sub will already know not to come into the session with expectations and surrender completely to you.

◆ ◆ ◆

How do you get a sub to surrender completely?

For me, the prerequisite to getting a sub to surrender truly is trust. If they feel safe with you, it's much easier to let go. Think of it like that exercise that you invariably did in camp or school as a kid: when you're taught to stand facing away from someone, yet completely trust that the person behind you will catch you when you lean back. That's all it is. If your sub knows that you're there for his best interest and can assuredly take responsibility for his well-being in the session, he will surrender.

How do you get someone to feel safe with you and trust you? Truly listen to them. Be open and operate from love and care. It helps to be relaxed and comfortable in session, because people tend to mirror the person they're with. Around an anxious or insecure person, we also feel anxious and insecure. Empathy goes a long way towards establishing this type of connection. If you already know what they're feeling and respond accordingly, that will help someone relax in your presence. A lot of trust is earned, too, so be aware that this can take time especially because a lot of people have underlying beliefs that others are not to be trusted. You may never know what people's unconscious beliefs are or even how they are formed. Even if you come up against someone's belief, just do your best. You never have to prove anything because a lot of times you can't change someone's filters no matter what you do.

◆ ◆ ◆

How many fetishes should I be familiar with?

Optimally, you want to build a broad knowledge base comprised of all fetishes and kinks, at least what they are and how they work. That way, you have more ways of integrating them, building a complex session and playing creatively with the interests of your client. It also gives you more opportunities to learn what you like and what you don't like. It can be embarrassing if the client asks for something and you have no working knowledge of what they're asking for. They're entrusting you as an expert in the field, so you need to have a professional approach and perspective even if it's: "I don't offer that," That being said...

◆ ◆ ◆

Is it better to have a specialty?

A bsolutely. It's better to be known for something so that the subs looking for that specific thing know where to go. It's easier to build a following and reputation that way. Early on, I learned that it was better for business to be able to do as many diverse scenes as you can. This may be true towards the beginning of your career, but no matter what, if you stay in this industry for a while, you're going to find that it gets more specific. I personally feel it's better to be great at one thing than it is to be mediocre at everything. You still need to understand how most things operate but that doesn't mean you have to do them all.

If you look around at the top indie dommes now, they all have a "thing". Some specialize in bondage, other in heavy corporal, some even specialize in specific types of clothing, like latex or leather. My recommendation would be to offer many things at first so that you have the chance to figure out what sticks. Then, as you collect empirical evidence for what works, what doesn't, you start to develop more in one, or a few directions.

If you pick a very niche and in-demand specialty, then this can build your reputation fast. As I mentioned before, there's probably a good reason why not many people offer it, so be sure this is something you're okay with and you've considered the long term effects.

I once read a study that women tend to be overqualified in too many things instead of being qualified in one or two things because it stems from a lack of confidence. It also said that by opting for the latter, people tend to achieve more success because it's easier to define, therefore cognitively easier for someone to comprehend. They'll remember, "she's into bondage" or "she's into heavy pain" and it's easier to explain to someone else, more than, "she does a bunch of things but nothing in particular sticks out".

◆ ◆ ◆

How much am I in control?

You want to be control all of the time during a scene. Many subs will try to override your control, and your toughest task is maintaining and negotiating the power. You want to be engaged enough so that it's still a dialogue, meaning, communication is still happening and you're open to your sub. Focus on your partner because he's half of the scene.

When I first began I thought that to be in control of the scene was to not only refuse, but negate, or wall-off the client when he wanted something, suggested something or attempted to subvert the power dynamic. Sometimes I'd get triggered and upset. Sometimes, anger is warranted, but remember if you get triggered it can come off as you losing control.

Here's an example: I used to have a sub that continually tried to push boundaries. He would try to grab my breasts or butt and tried to manipulate me to see him outside of the dungeon. He'd tell me what to do in the form of commands. One time, he told me to put on my shoes towards the end of the session because he wanted to look at me in my shoes. I got angry because it came after a slew of other demands and I frankly didn't want to be told to put on my shoes. I was more comfortable without them on especially carrying out some difficult labor at the time. The way he said it felt demeaning. So I asserted myself and said: "who's in control?" and he freaked out. The better way to have handled this would have been to either ask him: "you want me to put on my shoes? You'd like that wouldn't you?" in a playful, challenging way. You can even say, "so what will you do for me?". This puts the attention back on them, and you're still engaging without losing your power or closing off. One domme even taught me that you can agree to do something only if they will do something for you, which keeps the power on your side because you're deciding what the stakes are.

Another tactic would be to give a non-answer like a "maybe", instead of yes or no which is vague enough to suggest a possibility but doesn't lock you into anything. You can set up stakes too, like, "maybe, if you're a good boy," so that it incentivizes good behavior which can save energy for you in the long run.

◆ ◆ ◆

*Do you pre-plan your sessions
or go with the flow?*

I do both. At the very beginning of my career because I worried if I'd perform correctly, I used to plan out everything before a session. Then, as I got the dreaded mistress-itis, I stopped planning at all.

I feel it's necessary to maintain a good balance. You want to enter knowing a general structure based on what you know about your client already, but you also want to be open so that your intuition, or the present moment can guide you. Some things you can't plan for, for instance, if your sub breaks down or if you have a sudden creative impulse. Those are session breakthroughs in my mind. Too much reliance on plans will sometimes block those moments and instead of being outcome focused, you lose yourself is process. When you focus on the process, you lose sight of the overall picture.

Your subs will usually give you a great deal of information to go on. Some will even try to plan the whole session. Remember to respect their limits, but anything other than that is up to your discretion. You can take it into consideration but you are never beholden to it. Any sub who tries to convince you that you must follow everything exactly as they want it is not genuinely a sub. They're topping from the bottom.

At the moment, I usually get visions about what the session will look like before it happens. This started happening as I opened up my intuitive gifts. I'll usually clairvoyantly see or intuitively know what my clients will like before they tell me. I trust these intuitions wholeheartedly and allow the rest to flow through me in session.

Stay present, allow your sessions the room to breathe, allow movement in the scene instead of staying locked into something fixed. A good flow feels like an oxygenating breath, in and out, contracting and expanding.

◆ ◆ ◆

What is a good flow in sessions?

Y ou want to have a good pacing and be tuned into your sub as much as possible. You want to alternate positions and techniques throughout the session, but not so much that it's manic. I always tune into, and communicate with my sub to know when it's time to change. For instance, if we're flogging in one position, I'll notice if he seems tired through his body language (legs buckling, for example, although everyone shows fatigue differently) and we'll switch positions. With any corporal play, you'll notice that some people hit a certain point where sensation is dulled or they seem unresponsive to strikes because they've become desensitized. This is a good time to stop.

If it's a heavy corporal scene and marks are previously negotiated, it's a good idea to stop when the skin starts to change in texture. It starts to feel hard and almost rubbery when the area has had enough impact. With corporal, it's important to pace the scene so that you're striking, then massaging the areas too.

Intuitively, I try to balance my activities so that some are active and some are passive. For instance, if you've just finished caning someone, now is a time to switch to an activity like mummification instead of more impact play or anything intense.

The flow in every session is going to be different depending on your sub. Some people have a higher threshold for stimulus and want it for the excitement, while others need you to lead them into a more relaxed, tranquil state of being to escape their fast paced lives. I feel it's always better to switch up activities and do a few things per session than having it be just one thing that becomes route. This is the general rule I adhere by. There is an exception to this: some subs feel safer when play is predictable because they may feel anxiety if things change too much.

It may be a good idea to curate a playlist and work with the pacing of the music. This always helps the flow in session. This is by no means necessary. Sometimes my sessions are silent. Silence and sound can often be utilized as tools.

◆ ◆ ◆

How do I negotiate?

F irst, ask them what their limits and interests are. Then ask them for information about past experiences, if they have any. Some good questions to ask are:

"What did you like the most in past sessions?"

"What did you like the least?"

"How will I know that you're enjoying the session?"

"How will I know if you're not enjoying the session?"

"What are you hoping to get out of the session?"

"What injuries or physical limitations should I be aware of?"

Lastly, establish a safe word and let your sub know they can use this at their discretion. I generally use red and yellow because it's easy. Red means the scene terminates, yellow means back off a bit. You may even want to discuss the meanings with your sub because specificity matters. You can never overcommunicate on the safe word because you want to minimize miscommunication.

Remember, negotiation is not a deep heart to heart and it's not therapy. This is just to get vital information for your session and to establish rapport. That way, you don't interrupt the session flow to ask these questions during the session. You don't want to take up most of your session with a negotiation. Typically, they take about 10-15 minutes. **Remember, the session is action focused, not talk focused** unless it's a heavy verbal scene.

On that note, I once had a heavy humiliation scene during which my sub asked to cry. I went far with the humiliation and he did in fact cry, but he also terminated the session because he felt hopeless. Back then I had little experience and didn't realize that I triggered a few traumas for my sub because it was also my first time playing with him. To be fair, he didn't communicate any of his triggers to me, he just asked for me to make him cry. I felt terrible after even though one of the dommes said that I achieved the objective and therefore it was a successful session. The headmistress told me that in humiliation scenes it's best to still give a sense of hope. Verge on fun and light if you can. If you sense a weakness or insecurity, do not attack those unless it's a degradation scene.

What does aftercare look like?

A ftercare is comfort. It's essential for any BDSM session because of the intensity at play. Some of your subs will experience sub-drop, which is when they come down from the heightened charge of subspace. Others may have encountered an emotional trigger. Basically, aftercare is reassurance that you, their domme, is holding space for them, care and love them. If you don't engage in aftercare, there's an emptiness and vacuity to the session you don't want. It's like if you hook up with someone and right after, both of you put on your clothes and don't touch each other. That kind of distance may work for some people, but I'd guess that most people want some reassurance that they're safe and valued especially after such an intimate and vulnerable act.

You can hold or hug your sub. Check in and see if s/he is doing alright. Converse with him. You want to maintain the connection throughout the entire session, aftercare included.

There are some subs that may get off on the alienation of no aftercare, no acknowledgement after the session ends, but I don't often encounter them. There are subs that have a preference for a cold and rejecting experience, but I personally find this to be on the abusive and potentially damaging side. It's good to prioritize safety and healthy protocols.

◆ ◆ ◆

How do you know the session went well?

The sub will tell you so. Other times you'll never even know. I've had sessions I thought I messed up but later received a glowing review for. The best way to handle this is to do your best in every scene and know that even if your sub isn't happy with the session, that you know you put in your all. It's impossible to have every sub be happy with every scene you do. Sometimes the connection isn't right, other times there are variables you can't control like you or your sub had a bad day or you experience interruptions in your session you couldn't prevent. The only thing you can control is (if independent) who you see and your own performance.

◆ ◆ ◆

Should tribute stay an invisible piece in the equation?

I never count the tribute in front of my sub and in the dungeon we were told not to. However, there was a domme who did and I found it refreshingly transparent. It's up to you how you want to handle money in your sessions, there's no right or wrong. As advice, I'd say not to make your sessions about money unless you're a findom- it can be a transparent piece behind it all sure, but focusing on money without it being a tool in the power dynamic can be tricky to manage. In a general sense, in our world we understand that a person who has money in an exchange holds a certain amount of power. Especially if they're paying for a service, then, as we all know, "the customer is always right," which is saying in another way that the person paying holds the power. Many people play control and power games with money consciously and unconsciously in all different settings, not just this one. Any sort of power games played through money is the antithesis to the power dynamic that you as the domme, want to establish in the scene. That's why it's wise to minimize too much engagement with money unless it's a tool for the power exchange to be in your favor.

The trick to this is first flipping this script as much as possible in your own mind first. Whatever you believe in your unconscious will hold true in subtle ways. Know that you have something valuable to offer, know that the tribute is called a tribute for a reason: it's meant to be a devotional offering and a true sub will always know this. He will never try to make you feel smaller through money.

◆ ◆ ◆

What do you do if a ses-

sion goes wrong?

First thing: don't freak out. Be honest with your sub, but not in a way that makes him freak out either. At the beginning of my career I've had a few mishaps and luckily being in a dungeon meant I could ask for help during a crisis. If you rent out a dungeon as an independent, you'll also have staff on hand in case of emergency. Please use your judgement. If it's a life threatening emergency, call 911.

It's also good to get CPR training and have a first aid kit on hand.

In the case the session goes wrong in a different way, for instance, if your sub terminates the session, first don't take it personally. Take the time to ask them why, what happened and how you can fix it.

If you can't, I would just accept a loss and handle the situation in a gentle way. We've all had situations when we haven't clicked with someone who was providing something and in those situations we all know it's hard to speak up. I would even thank the person for taking care of themselves.

On the other hand if the person is just being an asshole then that's different. I'd try to get the person to leave as cleanly as possible even if it means placating them and warn other people from seeing him, or post an alert on verify him so other people know the situation. If you can help it, do not escalate the situation even if you want to. It's better to minimize risk in these situations that can become dangerous. Taking a loss here is better than provoking a hostile situation in which your physical safety could be threatened.

In the dungeon I had one session where there was no connection at all, and the sub wanted to end the session. During that time I was taught to take the time to talk with them and ask them if there is anything I can do differently. The priority here was to get the sub to agree to finish the session. Honestly, I'd rather refund their money instead of trying to force a connection or complete a subpar experience. The financial gain isn't worth the amount of energy loss it takes to finish a session like this. It's up to you to weigh your gains and losses.

◆ ◆ ◆

How do I cultivate a relationship?

I feel that a relationship naturally develops if there's a good rapport. Some dommes will tell you they want to make the sub dependent on them. I don't agree with this mentality because I come from a healing background where I want to cultivate agency and independence in each of my clients. I find that to be a healthier way of relating to someone because you're operating from integrity, not to mention your clients won't drain you like they will if they grow dependent on you. In the long run, this way of relating to my clients protects my wellbeing even if it may cost me money. I'd rather lose some money than come to hate my job.

It's good to be friendly, approachable and open to an extent. I feel that the power exchange dynamic offers some distance in between that's important to the dynamic. If you share too much or become too close, it's difficult to manage power.

Like all relationships, it's best to let things evolve organically. If there's a connection, it will develop over time unless someone is actively resisting it.

Is a slave relationship for me?

Slave relationships are very demanding. This is a full time, committed relationship that often starts with a contract dictating that the sub gives up certain rights. As the domme you control and monitor your slave and this can often be a 24/7 position. Sometimes in BDSM the word slave gets thrown around, or people are collared without building the proper relationship. It takes time and work to create a genuine slave relationship. It's real, like marriage and not to be something taken lightly.

I don't take slaves because I know the amount of energy it takes. I know what is expected of me and it's a lot more than I can commit. Also know that sometimes slaves can become needy because part of the dynamic is co-dependent, meaning, the domme takes responsibility for the slave in many ways and in its unhealthiest form it can be draining because you're sharing one source of energy.

If you're just starting out and interested in this route, it's a good idea to start with a slave who has experience in the past so that you can work out your own likes and dislikes with the slave guiding you. Once you've established your parameters and picked up basic protocols, then try it out with a slave who has less experience, one who you can train in your specific way.

When writing a contract, it can be fun to take away a lot of your slave's liberties, but remember that with every right you take away, you're also required to monitor it. Meaning, be careful not to overcommit. You're the one who has to make sure your slave adheres to what's in the contract otherwise it becomes a one-sided relationship.

◆ ◆ ◆

What happens if a sub/slave paid relationship becomes personal?

This happens more regularly than it's discussed. Dommes function in such an intimate space that this is likely to happen. In the past I've had three clients who took a personal role in my life as either a personal sub, friend, and once someone I dated. I would never date someone I met through BDSM ever again, as I now know it doesn't work for me (the client/ provider framework is a tough one to override) but sometimes if there's a very strong connection, where you met or how you met isn't of importance. They're meant to be in your life and you in theirs. Be prepared that if it becomes personal, most times it can never get back to professional.

I would urge you to err on the side of caution here. Unless someone has proven that they're really there for you and not trying to get close to you to get services for free, then don't allow them to have personal access to you. That being said, the dungeon is an interesting place to meet people you would never have the chance to meet otherwise, so revel in that too.

I once had a sub who really wanted to be my personal slave from the get go. I struggled with boundaries then and also felt an unconscious need to give everyone what they wanted from me. This sub, although kind, had many unresolved issues relating to his family that he pushed onto me. He was pushy, clingy, needy and demanding, wanting my attention and time at all times immediately. You could tell that he was trying to fill a void in his life and made me responsible for his happiness. It got to be too much and from that point on I stopped allowing anyone to have personal access to me unless it was a friendship that I initiated. If a relationship is getting too taxing for you, you reserve the right to walk away.

Sometimes walking away or setting a boundary, even if someone else feels hurt or angry, is the best thing you can do. Sometimes people need to have a certain number of people walk away before they recognize they need to change. **Remember, you have the right to say no.** Also remember that any relationship is a step by step process. Don't give anyone full access to you right away and never tell someone where you live immediately before you establish trust.

What is a service top?

A service top is someone who takes the "top" or dominant position in the session with the sub telling them what to do. So, although the service top seems to be in the position of power, the sub is actually the one controlling the session. The top is just taking orders or pleasing the sub by doing what she/he/they want. You can be a service top and be submissive, even if you're the top in the scene.

There are many professional dommes who act as service tops. They cater to their subs' wishes and desires without asserting their own control in the session, and it works for some people. It depends on how much you're willing to negotiate power and how much you want to make this service-oriented. I'd recommend you try both types of sessions, one in which you're a service-top and one in which you aren't and see how they fit you. There are successful pro-dommes out there who fit into both categories.

At the beginning of my career I was more of a service-top. That's how my dungeon expected us to be. We were kinky playmates more than real dommes. That style worked for them as they catered to their clients and that's the type of clientele they attracted: ones who topped from the bottom. As I grew, I grew less interested in being a service top. I haven't had someone try to top me from the bottom in years. That being said, even if someone isn't interested in topping from the bottom, many experienced subs will ask for things they like because men aren't conditioned like women. Women are told not to ask for things whereas men are encouraged to be vocal. Depending on what is asked, I'll assess if it's a reasonable request and meet or deny it based on my judgment.

◆ ◆ ◆

What is some safety advice for BDSM?

Never hit the kidneys and the neck up. Avoid the entire midsection on the back including the tailbone. Upper back and buttocks are the places to aim for during impact play. Don't hit the spine directly.

When tying someone, try not to elevate their hands high above their head for too long. This can make someone pass out if their circulation isn't great. When tying, watch the parts of the body that you tie. If these areas turn white or reddish purple, it's time to loosen the rope. Cutting off circulation for too long is never a good idea. Generally be aware of rope safety. Take bondage courses if you're going to practice bondage. There are nerves and arteries that, when compromised with bondage, can cause serious injuries.

If your client does pass out (none of my clients have ever passed out, but in the dungeon I've heard of many clients passing out with other dommes) position them on their back on the floor.

Obviously, when mummifying avoid the nose. When doing any sort of breath play, be sure to monitor the breath so that you don't accidentally suffocate them.

When engaging in any sort of blackmail, make sure you don't cause permanent damage to the person's life unless previously negotiated. In fact, with everything, make sure you don't take things too far. Practice integrity first and don't get carried away. Power can be intoxicating and having someone be your blank canvas to do whatever you want with them can lead to troubling behavior. Curb yourself.

Never compromise confidentiality unless the safety of either you or your sub is threatened. That means, even when talking to your friends, avoid sharing personal information about the sub. This is a small world, you never know who people know and what damage you could cause by gossiping. If you need advice about how to handle a particular situation with someone, you can share the details of the session but don't share the person's name.

◆ ◆ ◆

How do you make BDSM healing?

In my mind, BDSM itself is already healing. Although I won't go into how I work my magic in this book, I will say that if you practice BDSM in the right way, you can already create cathartic experiences and a chance for your sub to process emotions. In all ways, BDSM can be an antidote for toxic societal structures, so this is healing to both top and bottom as long as you engage with it safely and consensually.

◆ ◆ ◆

What is niteflirt?

N iteflirt is a phone sex service that a lot of dommes have. You can charge what you want and clients can call you and get charged per minute. You can also upload clips and photos to sell. niteflirt takes 30% of everything you make. Although it's steep, you do stand to profit from niteflirt because those minutes add up. Given that you have the ability to adjust your rates, you can factor in the payout to niteflirt if you want.

When I started on niteflirt I charged $3.99 per minute. Typically people charge around $2.99. I then continued to hike it up over the years. Although I get way less calls now, I feel like my time is better compensated. Clients don't typically call me for phone sex but for conversation or spiritual advice. I've had some lovely conversations over the years that I treasure. I advise you get this if it's something you can build into your business and link it on your website.

◆ ◆ ◆

Do I want to session with other dommes or independently?

I f you're doing classic BDSM and it's compatible with other dommes, then it's a good idea to take doubles, triples, etc. There are a lot of subs out there who want to book with more dommes because it adds to the stimulus, fun and humiliation. Not to mention, it can be very fun for the dommes involved. When I was still engaging in classic BDSM, I had the most fun in multi-domme sessions because it's like a party and you can bounce ideas off one another. It's a good way to get exposure to more clients who might have not met you otherwise. Sometimes they may not click with you online but when they meet you in person they realize there's a connection. The tricky part is negotiating different tributes if everyone is independent, because not everyone will have the same tribute. Sometimes it's easier to work out a standard tribute so that everyone gets paid the same.

How do you become successful?

L ongevity. If you can stay in the game and continue to build your skillsets, that already sets you apart from many of the dommes who try this out for a few months to a year and stop practicing. If you commit to this, are smart about your business and have a combination of natural and practiced skills, you will undoubtedly become successful over the course of a few years.

A core part of longevity is making sure that you're the amount of sessions that works for you. You may be able to get a lot of cash in a short amount of time, but if you're not thinking long term and making some sacrifices in the time being to preserve your energy, then you won't have a long term career.

To do this right it's best to have both short term and long term goals. You need to be happy in the moment with your career, but still investing in and considering the long term.

◆ ◆ ◆

Do I need to tell my family?
Does your family know?

No you don't need to tell your family. This is a personal choice. My family found out years ago and I'm still not sure how. My mother snooped a lot and may have found traces of my work and followed them. Luckily it wasn't the end of the world, even though I anticipated it would be. It was a good chance for me to practice not letting judgments get to me. It's a choice to carry shame, as it is a choice to let go of it too.

Some girls never tell their families. Others are open with their families. Many other dommes get "found out" the way that I did. If you plan on hiding your profession from your family, make sure you do it well and keep a low online profile. Just know that the longer you stay in this profession the more of a chance someone in your close proximity will know. Family especially, can sense when you're withholding information and they have the most re-sources to find out that information.

How do you come out to people in your life?

Nowadays I like to tell people right away. When I do, I feel relieved and feel like I can be myself, not to mention it saves me time. If I build a relationship with someone who I can't be truthful with or who will judge me, then it's a waste of time. If I'm upfront and they're accepting, then I know that's someone I want to invest time and energy into.

Tell them that you're a professional dominatrix and tell them that you don't have sex with your clients. The dungeon head-mistress advised me to tell guys I'm dating that it's for "artistic expression". I've never used that line before, but that's also something you could say. Most people I've told have been very accepting and curious about what I do. There have been times in the past when I felt judged, but don't take that personally. That only reflects their level of consciousness and open-mindedness. More on this later.

GENERAL ADVICE

When seriously considering whether I could be a professional domme, I asked: "do I need to speak in a certain tone?" I was worried that my voice wasn't authoritative enough. As high as my voice is now, before, it was even higher. The reason I asked this was because I started with a set idea in my mind of what a domme is, and should be. In my mind I narrowed down what I thought was appropriate and what wasn't. I already created a list of why I couldn't domme before I even tried: I'm too nice, I'm too soft, my voice is too high, I'm not dominant enough, I'm too shy, too caring. I fretted about the standards I may not be able to meet. Nothing was stopping me from starting the job except for me.

I've come across this checkpoint many times in my career. When considering to go independent, I seriously doubted my capabilities. It's a lot more responsibility to take on. I suppose in ways this is like a relationship and it's natural for people to freak out before they take the next step.

If you approach any self doubt, instead of thinking about all the reasons you can't do this, or anything in life, start thinking about what you can do.

◆ ◆ ◆

Lesson #1: Be true to you

Before I started domming, I'd of course seen representations of dommes in media. I remember in "Secret Diary of a Call-Girl", the main character invites over a domme. She was older, refined, cruel and so comfortable in her latex catsuit. Her slave followed her every barked order and whimpered every time she kicked him while he was under the table. I remember Almodovar's version of a domme in his film "I'm So Excited" (2003) who represented the bearer of high society secrets. She had a calculated, haughty presence. She wore trench coats and had a pristine hair cut like Anna Wintour. I thought that was what I needed to be to be a successful domme. Back then I was a 24 year old vulnerable mess. There was no way I could "get it together" enough to be like them. I couldn't even domme in my personal life. How could I ever be a pro?

Even if you don't have references, I'm sure you have some idea of what a domme "needs" to be like. When you do conjure up that version of a domme in your mind's eye, destroy it. Most of these versions of dommes aren't created by people who have experience in the field. One of the most foundational things is to go into this work with a blank slate and therefore, an open mind. An open mind looks for possibilities whereas a closed one looks for limitations. It will take you some time to find your particular voice, image and brand, but the more you can begin creating something for you, the better the outcome because your clients will already know what niche or specialty you occupy and therefore, what you offer.

If someone tells you you need to be one way, it's time to re-evaluate what they're teaching you because I would have a lot of questions about their belief systems. At the beginning of my career I was told I needed to grow out my hair, that I couldn't dye it, that I needed to wax/shave/remove all of my pubic hair. I was told I needed to be a certain weight and the headmistress would weigh me or comment that I'd gained weight if I just came back from vacation. I heard of and witnessed girls being taken off the calendar unless they lost a certain amount of weight. This is extremely toxic behavior because when it comes to fetish, diversity is celebrated and all bodies, all looks have a place. In fact, the more unusual you are, the more you are fetishized. If you fit into a prototype, you're replaceable.

The reason the headmistress wanted this from me was because she said clients want a certain predictability with your look. But my advice is this: BE YOU. If a client connects to YOU because you give them something to connect to, then they won't care if you change your hair one day. I say personality over image. A lot of these subs are looking for something surprising that their predictable worlds don't offer them. Besides, if you keep the same image for years and years, you'll get bored with yourself, and that boredom is something that will spill over into your sessions too. Your clients will get bored with you because they can sense you're bored with yourself.

Although none of the other women forced any image based advice on me, I did feel subconsciously pressured to adhere to "traditional beauty" i.e. growing my hair out long. I feel that there are some socially agreed upon traits that signify beauty, but I don't even think you need to be beautiful when you're doing this work. Sure beauty can help in any profession as it can open doors, but I feel outlook and attitude are truly the keepers. You want to hold attention, not just entice.

At the beginning of my career I did try to act like what I thought a domme "should" be, but that led to me being mechanical in session. I wrongly thought then that there was no place for me. I may be different from most dommes out there, but I can assure you that my distinct personality is not only alright, but valued. It's what sets me apart and that is what is irreplaceable. There can never be another you. Not to mention, the more you deviate from the stereotype, the more you're remembered because it's something unexpected, therefore, exciting.

Remember: if someone tells you to compromise your uniqueness, approach their advice with a critical mind.

◆ ◆ ◆

Lesson #2: The most important relationship is with yourself

T ake time to learn your own boundaries and don't be afraid to assert them. If you can maintain a good relationship with yourself, then your other relationships in this work will be good too. A good relationship with yourself means you make decisions that add to your self worth and confidence.

If you look at this work as a means to an end, with that end being money, you're much more likely to forgo your own personal boundaries and contribute to burn out. In this work, when you're first booking and aren't sure of where your boundaries are, many people will try to take advantage of that. They can sense if you're just after money too and will often try to offer money for different activities that may or may not make you uncomfortable. In this situation, they're using money to leverage power over you and it's power reversal that's not in your favor. If you accept, you've not only lost your power, but you may have compromised yourself and even if you don't register it consciously, unconsciously you may have lost some self-respect. It's these subtle choices that have real ramifications because they all add up. The opposite is true too. Small positive choices add up to a larger way of relating to the self.

For me, personal integrity is the most important part of my work, and within that is self-respect. Yes I've felt compromised when I first started, when I was more malleable, less sure of myself and less invested in the work itself. Luckily, what drove me in the work was my own fascination with BDSM and personal fulfillment. There have been missteps, but if you focus on those two motivations, you're adding to your self worth.

With social media, we may have many different illusory understandings of what domming is, how much glamour or decadence are available. What you may not see is that everything has strings. And you may be overlooking who's pulling those strings. Minimize strings at all costs and focus on you.

◆ ◆ ◆

Lesson #3: Domming is an art

J ust like with any other type of art, you may devalue a piece if you don't know how to appreciate it. Mastery of BDSM is mastery of many components: psychology, fantasy, power and all different types of specialties physical and otherwise. I don't think it's possible to have a true mastery of BDSM because there are way too many different specializations. I think it's possible to be a master of Shibari, a master of flogging, etc..If you come into this not willing to invest, then it's similar to renting an apartment and furnishing it with only cheap furniture. It does the job, yes, but it's going to break. You'd only do that if you knew you weren't planning on staying that long.

At the beginning of my career, it was appealing to work at a dungeon that leveraged the fact that it provided all tools and clothing so that us girls didn't have to buy them. This is appealing to a noncommittal frame of mind, and in my mind, the less I invested the easier it was to walk out of this. But as I started to grow, it became so much more important to own my own tools and outfits. My own tools were the ones I practiced on and felt comfortable with. I trusted their quality and learned how they moved on different parts of the body. My outfits became part of my image and part of yet another creative outlet of photo collaborations. It wasn't until recently that I really began investing. Sometimes it's hard for me to justify when I'm investing through buying materialistic things. It often feels static, like a dead end. But then I remind myself that part of this job IS the tools, the outfits. It's like being a doctor and refusing to get a nice pair of scrubs or a business man who isn't willing to invest in an expensive, custom suit. People take you less seriously if you're not willing to take yourself seriously. In the world we live in, image is a way people make a snap judgment as to how seriously you take yourself.

The more you understand that this is an art, the more willing you are to be comprehensive and build your understanding, appreciation and skills. That means, going to workshops, researching and developing your skillset and brand. *The more you understand this is an art, the more you understand that you are an artist. That's the defining characteristic that all dommes who make it, have. It gives you more power in mindset if you know you're a creator*: a creator of both reality and fantasy.

◆ ◆ ◆

Lesson #4: Understand your power,
but don't let it get to your head

I t's common to hear that the make it or break it point is the one year mark. This is when "mistress-itis" either grips you and forces you out, or you work out your ego. Mistress-itis is a term used in the industry to refer to the inflated sense of ego that some girls develop initially, basically interchangeable for a sudden bout of narcissism and entitlement. When you're suddenly worshipped constantly in the dungeon and given permission to do things you thought you couldn't all your life, it starts to go to your head. It's great to have confidence and this work can help you in building that if you treat it in the right way, but it can also have harmful effects that impact your life and relationships. When some people have mistress-itis, they tend to believe that they can treat everyone in the real world the same way they treat their subs in session. No, you can't. I've met other women who have mistress-itis and it's intense. I once had a therapist who termed this: "radical confidence". They feel like normal rules and behaviors don't apply to them. When dealing with people with radical confidence, it's like they feel entitled to invade all your boundaries. If they can't get what they want from the interaction, they'll try intimidation tactics that cross many lines.

In doing this work, it's important to understand that the power is something given to you in session because it's a power exchange. You can't just take it at will because that's an abuse of power. It's important to keep working on your ego so that your work isn't ruled by ego. This goes for all careers, not just this one even though it's especially highlighted in this work. When you've developed an inflated sense of ego, it can feel good for a moment until you realize how the rest of your life deteriorates. I remember when I first started, I felt like I owed no apologies to anyone, that I could do whatever I wanted and people were inconveniencing me by treating me like I was just a normal human being. I said and did whatever I wanted without thinking of the consequences, and it impacted my work because I forgot that it was, in essence, service work! As the headmistress explained, that's like walking into a job interview thinking you already have the job when really, you have to convince them to hire you.

That's the bottom line. This is still service work. That's not meant to be a disempowering approach, it's the reality. The more you work at it, the less it feels like service work. Still, you are not some supreme goddess that was just discovered within dungeon walls, and can suddenly emerge into the daylight with a bunch of super powers. That may be difficult for the ego to swallow. It's important to do counterbalancing here, and what helps is if you have a vanilla job too. I used to know a pro who'd been working for ten years and knew to juggle school and a job as a waitress with this work. She said that helped her level out the domming and that's why she was able to stay in the industry for so long. Balance keeps you sane.

This is general advice for everyone who starts in this line of work, but for those who also want to know how it falls in line with spirituality, I'd say that there's an even more refined level of counterbalancing here. The more I continue in this work, the more my persona precedes me. I get recognized on the street. With persona comes ego, yet with spirituality, there's a goal of dissolving, or at least being in control of the ego. I believe more and more in humility and although that may be counter to being a domme (which is in some ways, ruled by ego, or can be i.e. "worship me" mentality) I still believe there are people out there who understand that the person who can properly cultivate an attitude of humility in a world and industry ruled by ego is the one that truly deserves worship. Worship isn't about ego, although having ego makes worshipping easier to digest.

In this vein, it's even sometimes hard to identify what humility is. I used to think humility was on par with having low self esteem and not accepting compliments, but it's really not. It's hard to understand as a concept because we are in a culture and society that perpetuates "me me me!" mentality. It's become almost a necessity, as we are self-promotional and much of our business relies on narcissism. Celebrities are the most self promotional of all because they have to be. Humility is a sense that dissolves all of that. It's not a "I don't like me," mentality, it's not a "don't look at me" mentality, but it's a reflexive, "who am I? Aren't I part of all?" a diffuse, questioning that lives simultaneously inside and outside of self, thereby liberated by the state. Narcissism lives entirely within, and then externally as a self monitoring of the within-state.

Enough philosophizing, let's move on to:

◆ ◆ ◆

Lesson #5: First master the psychology and emotions

Many people may tell you differently, that it is about the tools and techniques first and foremost, but I believe that that's the icing on the cake. To be a good mistress, it takes first, being comfortable with the subject matter, understanding how power moves and transfers, and how to work with someone's psychology and physiology.

Understand limits first. You'll want to know limits on an individual level with each sub and within each session, but also in broader terms too. Understand the physical capabilities of the human body. You want to know what activities can be potentially life threatening and therefore, what your own limits are. Beyond the physical body, many people have emotional and psychological limits too. Have a basic working knowledge of people's triggers, including your own.

Anyone can learn techniques, but they don't drive the session. If it were only based around tools and techniques, the overall structure, the intimacy, the sensuality, the personality of the session would be missing. It'd just be one technique to the next greatly reducing the rhythm and soul of the session. I strongly believe a skilled domme could run an entire session with just her gaze.

When I first started out, we were trained in general skills. The headmistress used to tell us the importance of honing our skills, mentioning that one woman who used to work for her didn't speak any English, yet was consistently booked because she developed her rope tying skills to fill the whole session. At the time I wasn't as interested in expanding my BDSM skills so I looked to other ways to use up the session time.

What drew my fascination was the mental aspect. I liked understanding people's fantasies and how to get in their heads. I loved how unique each person's psychology was and that the only constant was that all session elements could mean different things to each sub. For example, a flogger could be a sensual tool for one person, and to the next person, it can represent pain. It's not at all about the setting or the tools or even the domme, sometimes. It's about what all these facets mean to the sub. For the domme, it's understanding and seeing this, then knowing how to elaborate on the meaning.

I came to realize that if you put the sub as the centerpiece and focus on the unique chemistry between you two in the session, then that greatly informs how the scene develops and what tools to use. *Remember: if you put the chemistry at the center of the session, then it can unfold.*

If you can run an entire session without any usage of implements, then it's a good time to be adding techniques to the arsenal too. Power exists in many forms, and if you can already wield it in one whisper, one glance, one touch, then the techniques add to that impact because the foundation of the session is already there. If you can't, then you're just relying on the tools and techniques, but the heart of the session is empty. You can even run an entire session in silence, so it's not entirely dependent on the words but your demeanor and energy. That brings me to the next point:

Lesson #6: What you bring to the session is what you get out of the session energetically

I never learned this in the dungeon, but most of what domming is is energy exchange. Think about the physics of handling a flogger or a single tail- you're putting in energy into the tools which creates the motion and the impact which is then received by the sub. Take this one level further into the metaphysics, and you'll realize that the energy you put in to each session is what creates the experience.

Yes, the sub also has energy too that greatly impacts the session since it's 50% of the energy, but as the dominant, you are the one controlling the flow of the energy. If you come into the session with low energy and no enthusiasm, then the sub is going to feel that and come out feeling drained, and not in a good, cathartic way. If you come into this enthusiastic, fun, vibrant, then the session will be infused with that too and the sub will leave feeling that, regardless of your skill level.

In the end, if we distill it to the very basics, this is about whether or not people can, and want to, spend time with you. It's important here to practice being contained, you don't want your whole life to spill into the session because this isn't about you. This is also the place to operate from a good, high vibration because if you are upset, anxious, depressed, that energy will feed into the session. So, get your affairs in order, or at least don't bring that into the session.

◆ ◆ ◆

Lesson #7: Commitment is key

I f you want to be successful at this, your heart needs to be in it. If this isn't motivating for you, people will sense it and that's the energy that will detract people from coming to you. Commitment is stability and like I mentioned before, you get out what you put in. Also, if clients sense that you're not serious, you're more likely to attract people who try to exploit that. Unconsciously or consciously, they may sense that you haven't invested enough into the territory and some will try to push you. I've had that happen on multiple occasions when I first went independent, because it was easy to tell that I was vulnerable. If you project a sense of centeredness, that's security in and of itself.

If you're not willing to risk all, then this isn't right for you. You may never have to be in the position to risk all, but that risk always exists. The arena might be gray area, but the choice is black and white. You can always walk out of the work, but you can never say that you never did the work. That being said, it all depends on how you relate to the work and how the people you want to associate with relate to it too. This work means different things to different people so the impact varies. If you want to try it for a few months to see if it's for you and discover that it's not, and if you happen to be someone who treats this as a very degrading thing to have done, then that shame will weigh on you for a long time. If you're someone who is casual about this, then you'll relate to this in your personal story differently. It's all point of view.

Remember: what you commit to grows, because your energy is focused. With manifestation, with physics, where ever your energy is directed (and the more of it is directed), the more movement there is in that particular area.

◆ ◆ ◆

Lesson #8: Take it seriously, but not THAT seriously

W hen things don't work out in session, I take it very hard. Starting out, one of my coworkers would tell me, "who you bring into the session is just an exaggerated version of you," That helped a lot because it alleviated a sense of pressure. You don't have to play a role "right" and you can be true to you, but it isn't REALLY you in the session, so no need to take everything so personally and just let yourself go.

This is a bit of a contradiction, I'll admit. There's part of this that is serious. You have someone's physical, emotional, mental (and for me, spiritual) safety in your hands for the hour(s) you're with them. If you're not taking it seriously, you can go wrong. But then again, there is a levity to this work too. We have to admit there's some humor and absurdity at times. I feel the best sessions are a blend of fun, seriousness, lightness and groundedness. That attitude would be best to permeate all of life!

This is another area where having a stereotypical version of domination would work against you. Although the dungeon wasn't the best place for me, I am thankful for starting in one because it allowed the exposure to so many different styles. Some cruel, cold, some ridiculous, weird and some so funny I laughed the entire session. When it comes to too serious, what I mean is that it's a restrictive mentality. It's like committing to a relationship but then fixating on every single thing in order to "make it perfect", or having a kid and helicopter parenting. We know these behaviors have the paradoxical effect of ruining what it is we have. Let go a little.

◆ ◆ ◆

Lesson #9: Know how to negotiate power

I'm very lucky in my sessions now to never come across people who try to top me from the bottom. My sessions rely on absolute submission and my subs know that going in. In the past it wasn't always like that and I had some subs who were bossy or wanted their way in sessions. Some even tried to get me to see them outside of the dungeon or would try to get me to tell them how much I made. These were invasive behaviors and just starting out you'll most likely come across them a lot. I used to get mad when people pushed too hard, but that unfortunately works against you because if you get emotional, then you've lost control.

As I already mentioned earlier, when negotiating power it's in your favor to keep the flow. When someone asks you to do something, you can ask, "you want me to do xyz? That would turn you on wouldn't it?". A question almost serves as verbal aikido, deflecting the energy and using it against your "opponent". It's a distraction technique more than anything, because while they're pondering on their answers, you can be figuring out your next move. If what they say lands on you and they can see that it affects you, then you've lost.

All this being said, go easy on yourself. Within the session if it's a seasoned sub, they know that the power goes to you. That's how they derive enjoyment from the session and it's a win-win. There are some real assholes that get off from testing you though and as long as you get better with vetting (unless this is what does it for you too) you won't have to be tested. If you're high volume and booking isn't in your hands, you're more than likely to encounter these people. The thing is, masculine socialization (varies by culture) and arguably, biology, will often teach men to invade boundaries. So even if your sub doesn't mean to, if they try to "man it up" in session, sometimes it can look like real asshole behavior even if they don't mean it to.

Sometimes if they have a crush on you they'll try to overcompensate and be extra "manly" to get you to like them. Sometimes, and speaking generally here based on a standard social conditioning, something about submission in front of a woman they want to date counteracts what they feel they need to be in order to be attractive, so that's why there's a tendency to overcompensate. When a man is attracted to a woman, even in his body language he tries to seem bigger and more dominant, often pulling back his shoulders or putting his hands on his waist. You see this in the animal kingdom too. Peacocks spread their feathers. Submission itself counteracts tenants of traditional (toxic) masculinity even though I feel a man who can submit makes a truly strong man.

I remember a tender moment I shared with a sub once. He came to realize he liked me after we sessioned together. He asked, "will you still respect me after you saw me like this?" I told him, "I respect you more,"

◆ ◆ ◆

Lesson #10: Watch out for Ego Massaging

There's a fine line between worship and manipulative ego massaging. Sometimes clients will make appeals to your vanity or other attributes not because they're trying to worship you as per the session, but because they want something. It is such an easy way to pull the wool over someone's eyes and tip the scale in the sub's favor. Maybe it's as simple as wanting you to do "more" in the session or to allow them to do something that you've listed as a limit.

The first time I saw this happen was in doubles at the dungeon. I knew that the sub who came in was after something: access to more photos. The other domme in the session with me was the in house photographer, so he continued to massage her ego until she softened enough for him to then ask about photos, costs, and how he could get his hands on them privately, bypassing bureaucracy and an overcharge.

Especially in the beginning of getting to know a sub, it's good to be cautionary. This is exchange based and because of that, some-times both sides even if subconsciously, are assessing how much they can get out of the situation when there isn't true intimacy and trust in place. Especially since many of the clients are going to be people who work in business and finance, many of them will use negotiation tactics and assess outcomes so it's good to come into this work with a few guards up, allowing them to dissolve as someone earns your trust.

Lesson #11: Know your projections

With any type of work such as this that deals heavily with archetypes and power, transference will always happen. Just like in therapy, many people will choose therapists that remind them of people in their lives they want to work something out with. Teachers and professors get this as well. When you're a domme, you're more in the line of fire for this to happen because you are already in the "controlling matriarch" box. This means, be prepared to handle mother, big sister, boss, teacher transference. It can't get more obvious than in the role plays where you're actually playing out these archetypes. Where else than in BDSM is it more okay to call people "mommy" and "daddy" and have these dynamics integrated consciously and unconsciously?

I remember watching a documentary called "Fetishes" (1996) which followed dommes in Pandora's Box in the early 90's. In one interview, one of the dommes said that all dommes have a nurturing quality about them that remind their clients of moms. She said you couldn't do this job unless you had that quality about you. I strongly agree. Sure there are the "bratty princesses" of the domme world that have nothing nurturing about them, but I wonder how many of them are seriously invested in this career to be one of the greats. All of the world renowned dommes I know of have something nurturing, maybe even tough-love, about them. Something where, you immediately both trust and fear them.

I myself am a mommy domme. I have innately nurturing characteristics, and as someone who parented my own parents growing up, I always gravitated towards the role of caretaker with many of my friends too. I noticed that many of my subs were, and are, littles- or find in me something nurturing that reminds them of their own moms for better or worse. When you're a mommy domme, it is tricky territory because you not only trigger your littles more than anyone else, but they also unconsciously want you to take on an important role in their lives as protector too that may or may not extend past session time.

◆ ◆ ◆

Lesson #12: Take nothing personally

L ike the above, a lot of what comes out of the session or relationship hardly has anything to do with you. People are generally working through their own life. In such an intimate space as BDSM, you may invariably trigger someone at some point as all close relationships tend to do. The opposite is true too. A sub may trigger you in some way. As with all of life, if you take nothing personally then life and work are easier. Give yourself gentle reminders to detach from the job. Breathe a little. Have a glass of wine and a bath.

◆ ◆ ◆

Lesson #13: Try not to date your clients

A s I mentioned earlier, it's common for subs and dommes to develop personal relationships. From my personal experience, it's best not to date your clients or develop romantic feelings for them. Friendships are easy to navigate, but romantic relationships that start from the BDSM space are not. There are so many barriers in the way because chances are the sub is hiding this part of his life from his "real" life, because if he wasn't then he wouldn't be paying for it. A client-provider relationship becomes hard to shift when it turns into a romantic relationship. The power dynamic becomes difficult to juggle too. Because you may already know what turns them on. If you're not into that and they ask you to do whatever it is they like in your personal sex life, you may end up feeling used. That being said, I have heard of successful relationships that pro-dommes have had with clients, ones that weren't even kinky. From personal experience, the one time it happened for me got messy and I wish I'd kept to my boundaries.

◆ ◆ ◆

Lesson #14: Be patient

T he business portion of this takes a long time to build and the skills take a long time to master.

With regards to business, in my experience it takes time to build a business model that works for you. It takes time because a lot of building a strong foundation depends on trial and error. What works for someone else is not always going to be what works for you, so be open to experimenting and "failing" a few times before you find what works.

Skills take practice. It also takes time to find what skill sets appeal to you, that you want to continue to develop. It's been years and still I'm always learning new things, refining old things, and seeing what I want to integrate into my session structures. Patience is the precursor to perseverance. Luckily, if you find you really love this job, then patience comes naturally.

This reminds me of the classic marshmallow experiment conducted by Walter Mischel. Children were placed in a room and given a marshmellow. They could eat it or choose not to, which would earn them another marshmallow. The children who could delay gratification through distracting themselves were later shown to have "better life outcomes". Most times, it pays to perservere.

◆ ◆ ◆

Lesson #15: Wear what makes you feel both comfortable and powerful

Much of this is visual and some subs are going to have specific clothing fetishes. The good part about being indie is that you get to select your wardrobe, so even if a sub likes latex, you can choose within your own latex collection. That means you never have to wear something that makes you feel uncomfortable.

Always wear things that make you feel good in session, never things that are just to please your sub or to seem "sexy". Trust me, one of the most important parts to how you feel in the session is how confident you feel in your clothing. It's better to wear something that's not as flattering as long as you exude power, than it is to wear something you think is sexy that makes you feel uncomfortable and nervous. **Remember: power is presence is confidence is calmness. Any anxiety is the opposite of where you want to be.** For women especially, anxiety and "shrinking" in body language (which by nature is the opposite of power. A powerful presence is expansive) shows when she doesn't feel good in her body, skin and clothing.

◆ ◆ ◆

Lesson #16: Balance service and empowerment

It's a good idea to be aware that you do occupy a liminal space between service and empowerment. The more comfortable your mind is with holding these paradoxical states, the better. Yes we are being paid, and yes we still have autonomy. I believe that empowerment in this space is a mental state of acceptance. Since my communication is clean and my subs know that I will consider what they want but that it is up to me to execute what I feel is good and necessary, that takes care of the service expectations.

You need to find your power first in yourself and in your own life before you can feel empowered in this space. If you're not tapped into your own power, then power exchange will feel awkward and lopsided in the session. That's when you're more likely to go to extremes (abuse of power, or powerlessness).

Like in any healing or coaching, you learn that what you try
to find externally are really qualities you need to develop from
within. For example, people who look for romantic partners that
"complete" them, or have qualities they don't have yet want, are
attracting a partner out of a void. The absence of the desired
quality is what motivates the person to find someone to "fill it"
and that then creates a wound in the relationship because the un-
healed wound in one or both of the individuals is what is causing
this. It is said that you need to first develop those qualities in
yourself before you feel whole and healed, and therefore can attract a partner who is also his/her/their own person.

In applying this to BDSM, if you feel disempowered in your real
life, sure it can be a necessary and exciting outlet to come into
the dungeon and feel powerful. But if you already operate from
empowerment and come into the dungeon with that feeling, then
the power exchange will only heighten your wholeness. Instead
of creating a codependent relationship with your job or filling a
void in your life with BDSM, you come at it with your whole self,
which changes the game entirely.

People can always tell when you approach something because
you're trying to fill a void. Lack attracts lack.

◆ ◆ ◆

Lesson #17: Minimize "sexual services"

I realize this section may be inflammatory because domming
does sit in under the umbrella of sex work and many of you
are interested in domming in a sexual capacity. Based on my

experience, I feel that it's best to minimize what you offer in terms of sexual services. Domming is meant to be an experience in power play, in the mind, in my opinion. If the focus is purely on getting someone off, it reduces the impact of the work itself and can lead to burn out or escapism. Not to mention, it puts you at risk with the law, especially at present time.

Sexual services that are illegal, depending on state, include anything that's penetrative. Even if someone touches your butt or breasts, that is considered prostitution in NYC. In my work, I don't allow anyone to worship any part of my body except for my feet and sometimes my legs. I don't touch genitals in a sexual way (i.e. handjobs) nor do I allow my subs to orgasm whether that be on their own or with any sort of assistance like a vibrator. I set my limits this way because I'm not interested in sexual gratification.

Within the industry, I have noticed that there's sometimes a hierarchy. Many established pro-dommes seem to harbor some judgment towards escorts, or women who are dommes and tie that into escorting. My thinking on this is that withholding sex is a power play in itself, one that many dommes take very seriously. The dynamic is established because of its roots in who is wearing the phallus, who is penetrating. Because in traditional domming, some women use strap-ons. The person who is being penetrated is in the position of submission and power-lessness. If you are an escort and being penetrated, it can off-set the dynamic in a strange way. That seems to be the prevailing attitude in the US from what I've seen first hand and read, however in Europe this attitude seems to differ.

To reiterate: prioritize your safety at all costs. You can't and shouldn't do this work if you are not safe.

❖ ❖ ❖

Lesson #18: Domming is a great

chance to free yourself from
harmful conditioning

Society often tells you what you can and can't do as a woman. Then it tells you what you need to feel shame for. From the beginning, domming allowed me to rework these ideas. My first session involved a golden shower. I had so many notions of urine being shameful or disgusting. It was inconceivable to me that it was part of a session. Slowly, through exposures like this, I started becoming more open, adventurous and less judgmental about myself and about being human in general. A lot of social appropriateness locks us into ways of behaving and thinking that create chaos and loss of power within. When we realize that we're more free than we think, we release shame, fear, anxiety and resistance. We start to have breakthroughs and allow ourselves to be more in touch with our nature.

I started learning that how I was taught to be with men, overly giving and submissive, the "good wife"/"martyr" type, was not how I needed or even wanted to be. My mom taught me that women always had to be the do-ers, that to receive was to be selfish. I learned that it was okay to receive a little through domming. Yes the sub is relying on you to direct the session, but sometimes some subs truly just want to cater to you because they experience compersion when you're happy. BDSM opened me up to many different structures of relationships and dynamics, not just the heteronormative one I was conditioned to believe was the end all be all.

If you approach BDSM in an open way, it will bring up a lot of questions for you about yourself and your relationship to the world. This in turn can enrich your relationship to yourself. If we question, that means we stay in touch with our curiosity. If you look at some of the most successful people in the world, they all have one attribute in common: curiosity.

If you find yourself up against resistance or fear when it comes to certain exposures in BDSM, it's a good chance to grow. This job will push your limits and test you. The real test is if you allow it because if you do, you stand to grow a lot (my advice: allow your job to, but don't allow your subs to).

◆ ◆ ◆

Lesson #19: Put your integrity first

There are going to be many times when your integrity is tested, especially since you'll have power. Just because you have power doesn't mean you have the right to abuse it or exploit anyone. Even in situations when you have an advantage, it's best to act with integrity. Make sure you're putting out quality work, make sure you're being honest, make sure you're not taking advantage of anyone. With the veil of an alternate persona and reality, sometimes we can be de-personalized and cause harm to others. Try to snap yourself out of this if you sense this happening. It's okay to de-personalize your sub by making him wear a hood because he's not in the position of authority. De-personalizing someone in the submissive position can add to subspace. However, de-personalization in the position of authority can be a scary thing. Consult the infamous Stanford Prison Experiment by Philip Zombardo to see what people are capable of when they are de-personalized and in positions of power.

Karma exists and every action you take will come back to you whether acting from good or bad will. If you follow the path of integrity, then things are going to be a lot smoother. Sometimes, it's hard to act with integrity in situations when you don't know any better, or you had a positive intention going into. During those times, use the situation as a lesson for how to act in the future. I find that if you act very sales-y or upsell, you may benefit at the time but it's not acting with integrity and it will bite you in the ass in the long term. What more is that if you're being shady, you're going to attract clients who are shady too. It's the law of attraction.

There was one time in my whole career that I wasn't acting with full integrity. It was a situation in which my friend let me use his space to session for free, but because I wanted to compensate him as a gift I mentioned to my sub that there was a facility fee. This was the same time that my sub ended up not paying me at all and I lost over $1k. The universe taught me a lesson that day. No matter how insignificant the situation, your intention is what magnetizes the same intention back to you.

Remember: what you're investing in long term is reputation. You don't want a reputation as an exploiter or abuser. People come back to you ultimately because they can trust you and you provide a good service.

◆ ◆ ◆

Lesson #20: What you learn in a commercial dungeon is NOT real BDSM

I alluded to this lesson many times already. If you choose to start in a commercial dungeon, you'll most likely be taught how to be a kinky playmate, not how to be a real power player. In the dungeon you're taught how to perform route activities in a way that's like fast food. It might hit the spot, but the nutritional value and production are dubious.

If you plan on taking this career seriously, know the difference. Understand what you're learning and what you need to supplement. Understand that what you learn in the dungeon is not the end all be all. It's barely the start. Sometimes the only thing distinguishing a successful indie domme and an unsuccessful one is motivation.

◆ ◆ ◆

Lesson #21: Dommes need to supplement their income

You may not make a lot of money as a domme, but you will, like anyone who works for him/her/themselves will have more free time and control over your schedule. Most dommes these days need to supplement their income with clips or side businesses. Bookings can be erratic too, even in established dungeons. Sometimes you'll have an influx of clients, other times none. Especially if you book super selectively like me, sometimes months can go by and you won't work.

Be prepared to be creative with this work. Live sessions won't pay all the bills, but if you work smart and branch out, create a brand, then you can live off of it. I like the idea of diversifying my income stream, although many other people might like to focus on one thing at a time so that they can get the most out of it. If you come into this wanting a lot of money doing minimal work, then this is definitely not the best option for you.

Lesson #22: This will affect
your dating life

One of the first things I learned from the head mistress was that this would affect my dating life. She told me to watch a movie about a pro-domme called "My Normal" (2009). The main character started dating another woman who said she was alright with her job, but as feeling started developing, her girlfriend's attitude changed too. The same thing was told to me by one of the dommes who'd been in the work for 5 years. She said, they may say they're okay with it to start, but you can tell sometimes that changes.

Towards the beginning I noticed that the men I was dating, when I told them, either trivialized it or were entertained by it. They either acted dismissively towards it or tried to shame me because they thought that they weren't "weird" like me or my clients. A few asked a bunch of questions like, are you into it? What turns you on about it? What do you do in session? It was fascinating to me because they were so interested in it for people who were so attached to their self-proclaimed "definitely not kinky" identity, whatever that means. In psychology, I learned that it's the people who have a lot of resistance to one identity that usually are that identity. There was a study that showed people who are homophobes are more likely to be gay themselves.

I've had other men who were in more artistic industry treat it as something that added clout. They would tell all their friends they were dating a dominatrix because it was an exotic and "cool" thing.

Clearly I didn't appreciate either. I don't want someone to exoticize, fetishize, or overlook my profession as if it were a blemish. I then stopped telling people I was dating, but that created a barrier and I didn't like hiding or lying. I came to realize that I wanted to be with someone who not only accepted it, but approached it with no pre-conceived notions and appreciated it the way I did.

There were other men who seemed interested in it, but were really interested in collecting inspiration for their own work. As I grew more comfortable with myself, I started telling people right off the bat. Because of a lot of self-work I did, I also began meeting people who were more open minded and conscious because they were matching me on that vibration. Most if not all of those people were very open to it, fascinated, and appreciated me as a person and my philosophy. Not to mention, a few people even recognized it took tremendous bravery to do what I do and to choose a life off the beaten path. Those are my people. I wouldn't have found them if I didn't start being more open about it.

In the end, it's really about how much can you accept this in your own life.

I later started meeting more dommes who were married or in healthy relationships that were either kinky or vanilla. I know it can be done, and I'd advise that you just tell people right away. Hiding things never facilitates healthy communication, not to mention lying or withholding can be toxic to your health. Whether others accept it or think it's weird is not on you, but it can be valuable information for you so that you don't waste your time on them if they're not right for you. In the end, we want to know we spent time with the right people who loved us for us, don't we?

◆ ◆ ◆

Lesson #23: Keep subs beneath you

Taller people are perceived as more authoritative. Think back to all authority figures in your life you respected. You might realize that you think of them as taller, even if they physically were not. That's because our brains relate authority with height. In BDSM you can use this to your advantage by making sure your sub is always lower than you. If you're sitting, he's kneeling. If you're standing, he's still kneeling, or sitting. That's why heels can come in handy even if both of you are standing. Save moments you both are standing for the end of the session when you're saying goodbye and there's no need for a power hierachy. I usually have them kneel the second they step into the room before a session.

This same trick applies to all of life. I've noticed that even without a power dynamic, people are more likely to accept my advice if I'm "above" them, physically. I believe this happens because when you're a child, you're always looking up at your parents so when someone is higher than you, it still resonates with an infantile part of our brain.

◆ ◆ ◆

Lesson #24: This might begin to close you off in your vanilla life

I call this the *veil of secrecy effect*. As you grow in BDSM you tend to close off in your "real" life because you do work in a field that's secretive. Even if you learn to be open about it like me, you still won't want to come out to everyone all the time. I am selectively open with people I want to get to know, but in larger groups I feel it's better to avoid exposing yourself. Plus, I tend to feel like whenever you "out" yourself, the conversation becomes about you. Most times I don't want that type of attention.

Even if in larger groups you don't tell anyone, most people will be able to sense that there's something you're hiding, or, that something a little different or mysterious about you. They register this unconsciously.

I didn't even realize this was happening until it was brought to my attention by several people, namely my acting coach. It took a lot of hard work to unlearn this, to break down the barriers and walls that form because not everyone can appreciate the work you do. I advise that you consciously try to counterbalance this effect, so that you can be approachable and open with most people. Not everyone needs to know everything, but that doesn't mean that you constantly have to hide or protect yourself. That's operating defensively and a preventative attitude will often register as closed off.

To counterbalance, I often consciously remind myself to open my heart. This can happen through meditation or through making choices to facilitate more intimacy with the people in your life. That means honest communication, vulnerability and being more loving to others and yourself.

When you're operating from a defensive position, it's often because there's an inner instability. Maybe you don't feel that you 100% have "got you". Once you do feel like no matter what other people feel or think about you it can't touch you, that's when you're in an expansive, open state. That's when you're operating out of self love and self worth and my goodness does that open you up to abundance.

Lesson #25: Remember the value of money

When you're being paid in cash immediately and often in larger sums than you would get working hourly at a vanilla job, money can seem easy to come by. We can sometimes lose sight of the true value of money and overspend.

Find a way to keep yourself in check. You may be getting paid better per hour, but that doesn't mean that you should be spending all of it just as fast. You're still working for your money, just in a different way than you may be used to. In fact, realize how much effort it took to earn your cash: much more attention span than it takes for you to punch in some numbers on an excel sheet.

Lesson #26: Sessions teach you to be present

After working at an office job, the first thing you may notice with domming is how present you're forced to be. You can't have your phone in session (or at least I hope you don't!) and you're required to stay so engaged. Time starts to have a different meaning. You're "on" in a way you may never have been before.

In this technology era, this is a vital lesson. I suddenly learned how to truly be present when we as a collective as so used to being checked out and on our phones. Especially if we come from a full time job, we may be used to trying to "seem busy" or having our eyes glaze over on a computer since we're being compensated for our time in a way that doesn't require us to be present all the time. Suddenly in session, we come to realize that if we're not present, then we're not working.

This new mentality seeps into all areas of your life in a positive way. Afterall, we can only receive all that life has to offer us in the present moment. This moment is the convergence of everything, as we only make sense of the past and future here.

◆ ◆ ◆

Lesson #27: Don't push a pencil through a pinhole

I know what you're thinking. No, this isn't advice about strap ons.

My friend once said something similar to "don't push a pencil through a pinhole" and I found it to be such a valuable lesson. Even though I'm loosely paraphrasing the idiom, the meaning was the same. The idea is, don't make something bigger than it needs to be, including a relationship with a sub, or with anyone. Sometimes it's better to cut your losses if you're not feeling it, especially if someone's trying to force intimacy on you.

Back in the day I felt the need to deepen relationships with people who wanted more from me even when I didn't want more. I felt like I owed them something, or felt bad for them so I'd spend a lot of energy and time trying to communicate with them. I wanted to make sure they didn't feel bad or rejected and always prioritized taking care of them.

This had the paradoxical effect. These people felt closer to me and expected more from me. In all situations, it's best to take a step back and evaluate if this is something you want to pursue. Most times you'll find that it's better to leave something as it is. If you push a pencil through a pinhole, it only deepens and widens the original form when it might have been better the way it was intended.

◆ ◆ ◆

Lesson #28: This will change you

All in all, this work changed me in ways I wanted, in ways unexpected and in ways that were sometimes harmful. With a career like this, it's like a high risk investment, but it's one that I'm glad I made. Domming was essential in my own self-discovery and healing process. If it's calling you, then it's something that is worthwhile to explore because maybe there's something you need out of it like I did. Even if it's not for as long of a time as I put into it, maybe it's a bridge to something else. We can never belittle that possibility. I say life is too short to work a boring job or to not explore what resonates. When we follow resonance, we can get closer to purpose and meaning. That's what all of us want, deep down, isn't it? The human condition is constantly seeking answers for why we're here. Until we find the real reason, the purpose of life is finding that reason.

Lesson #29: Cultivate beginner's mind

Beginner's mind is a Zen Buddhist term I first came across in Aikido. The idea is, no matter how advanced you are, you need to continue approaching things with the open mindedness of a beginner. That means, you stay adaptable, you stay curious, instead of closing down or allowing your ego of "I know what to do," speak for you.

This is so important in this work especially as you begin advancing. Every client, every domme, every person you encounter can teach you a valuable lesson that can transfer into your own practice. If you remain locked into one way of doing things, you stop seeing that there are a multitide of ways to achieve the same aim.

You may have a set methodology at some point in your career, but remember that adjustments are always necessary. When times are changing as fast as they do now, to stay in the game you need to flow.

◆ ◆ ◆

Thank you for supporting me, for reading my words. I hope that you stay safe in your journey and take good care of yourself. The more that we can approach this work with positive intentions, the more we can broaden its reach and impact. I hope that we collectively can all learn to see that there's so much light, even in darkness. The true kind of light is only found in darkness.

To all of you who actively face your fears. I'm so proud of you. I feel that it's the bravest move of all. Most people are afraid of looking within because they don't want to face who they really are. For those of you who want to move closer to the truth, you are the ones that find the real gifts. The resilience, the strength and the power.

Keep on shining, brave souls. Someone's gotta do it and I hope it's you.

xo Aleta

Printed in Great Britain
by Amazon

57927938R00070